The Ramen King Ivan Cookbook

IVAN McCOMBS
A.K.A. @RAMENKINGIVAN

HARVARD
COMMON
PRESS

Quarto.com

© 2024 Quarto Publishing Group USA Inc.
Text © 2024 RAMFAM PRODUCTIONS LLC
Photography © 2024 David K. Peng

First Published in 2024 by The Harvard Common Press,
an imprint of The Quarto Group,
100 Cummings Center, Suite 265-D, Beverly, MA 01915, USA.
T (978) 282-9590 F (978) 283-2742

The Harvard Common Press titles are also available at discount for retail, wholesale, promotional, and bulk purchase. For details, contact the Special Sales Manager by email at specialsales@quarto.com or by mail at The Quarto Group, Attn: Special Sales Manager, 100 Cummings Center, Suite 265-D, Beverly, MA 01915, USA.

28 27 26 25 24   1 2 3 4 5

ISBN: 978-0-7603-8820-4

Digital edition published in 2024
eISBN: 978-0-7603-8821-1

Library of Congress Control Number (LCCN) available.

Design: www.traffic-design.co.uk
Photography: David K. Peng
Food Stylist: Christiane Hur

Printed in China

I dedicate this cookbook to everyone who got in trouble for playing with their food. This cookbook proves that playing with your food is not only fun, but it can lead to some really interesting recipes!

I would also like to thank my mom for creating the OG Ramen recipe. Without it, I wouldn't have had the encouragement to do it better!

To everyone who helped make this possible: Thank you so much for the support. I wouldn't be here without you guys.

Contents

Introduction

Welcome to the RamFam!

RamFam! Welcome to the cookbook you've been asking for!

I started this cooking journey—cooking seriously, and for a living—in 2020 when everyone was stuck in the house with nothing to do. One day, I found a cookbook with a bunch of prison ramen recipes, and I thought, *Why not make a video about it?* So I did. After posting that recipe on TikTok, I tried a few more and figured all this ramen cooking was just a way to entertain myself and, well, make a meal. Then, one of my viewers commented with a request for ramen lasagna (page 111), and that video went super viral! Everything changed after that day. Invites came from TV shows, people wanted to interview me, and the Ramen King came to life.

It's crazy how life works!

Before ramen, I was just a college graduate working at a regular company, clocking in and out but unhappy and unchallenged. Like many people, I wanted to do something that I believed in and that would inspire me, but I couldn't quite figure out what that looked like. Social media was a side interest, and I set up eight or ten different accounts, attempting to create something beneficial to a community because that was important to me. Truthfully, I almost gave up, but then I tried that ramen recipe, and the rest is history. Who knew that 2:00 a.m. hunger pangs could launch a new life path and bring together an incredible group of supporters?

So while some people look at my videos and dismiss them as just me acting crazy while creating weird recipes, I've built a community that I love called the RamFam! And we're not just making ramen. RamFam is about respecting each other and encouraging people to be better versions of themselves—that's my overall goal. I'm happy to share these recipes and excited for you to try them; apparently, I go too fast in my videos, so now you can relax, read, and know exactly how to make the dishes.

We're always told not to play with our food. But as you go through this cookbook, you will find that playing with your food couldn't be more fun!

What Is Ramen?

Ramen is more than the inexpensive packets stacked up in every dorm room and kitchen cupboard; this Japanese noodle soup has come a long way from its street-food roots. Fine-dining restaurants now have ramen on the menu because of its versatility and easy preparation. Ramen basically has three parts:

1. **Noodles:** Slurping the noodles is the fun part of ramen for most people, and they provide much of the bulk in the dish. Any kind of noodle can be used, and I will explain them in detail in the Types of Noodles section below.

2. **Broth:** Although the noodles often take center stage, the broth is the base of the dish. A truly delicious ramen starts with a delicious broth, which flavors the noodles. Professional ramen chefs have signature flavoring bases for their creations, and my recipes often play with unusual broth ingredients.

3. **Toppings:** Pretty much anything can be a topping for ramen; I'm partial to soft-boiled eggs (page 29), scallions, and sriracha, but options include other proteins, veggies, sauces, dumplings, and fruit. The toppings are arranged on top of the noodles to make an attractive presentation. The combinations are almost endless.

Types of Noodles

I don't use all these noodles in my recipes, but you can. It really comes down to what you have in your cupboard and your preferred texture. If you stick to ramen packages as the base of the dish, then the noodle choice is taken care of, but when you have time to play with your food, branch out a bit and experiment with others.

Ramen Noodles

The ramen noodles you are probably familiar with are made from wheat flour, water, salt, and kansui, an alkaline water containing potassium carbonate and sodium carbonate. This water is what gives ramen noodles their yellow color, unique flavor, and bouncy texture. It also impedes liquid absorption, so the noodles don't get soggy sitting in the broth.

Wait a minute, you might be saying—my ramen noodles are often soft, so why is that? Well, if you boil the noodles longer, they get softer. There are even names for the various boiling lengths in Japanese:

- harigane (extra-extra firm)
- barikata (extra firm)
- katamen (firm)
- futsuu (medium)
- yawa (soft)
- bariyawa (extra soft)

I like my noodles firm, but you can adjust boiling time to make yours perfect for you.

Sōmen Noodles

I use sōmen noodles frequently in my recipes; when I'm not taking ramen blocks out of the package, this is my first choice. Sōmen are thin, pale noodles made of superfine wheat flour, water, and salt. The dough is hand-stretched, and the noodles are coated in vegetable oil so they don't dry too stiffly. Sōmen cooks quickly, in about 3 minutes, and is delicious hot or cold.

Udon Noodles

Udon noodles show up in a couple recipes in this book as part of ramen or soup kits. They are also made with wheat and add a chewy texture and bulk to your ramen. Udon comes in various widths and are available fresh and dried. Because udon is thicker and broader, the cooking time can be longer than the thinner noodles.

Soba Noodles

Soba noodles are a bit like sōmen noodles, but they're thicker and made with buckwheat flour, so they're brown. Sometimes, white wheat flour is mixed in so the noodle is firmer, but check the label to make sure your noodles are 70 to 80 percent buckwheat for an authentic product. Soba noodles can be gluten-free if made 100 percent with buckwheat flour (juuwari soba), and they are higher in fiber and protein than any other Asian noodles. They have a slightly nutty flavor, which goes well in any of the recipes in this book.

Rice Noodles

Rice noodles are made with rice and water and come in a variety of widths and lengths, as well as fresh or dried. They are gluten-free and cook much faster than wheat-based noodles. You can soak them instead of boiling them, then just throw them in your recipe near the end to heat them up. Never boil fresh rice noodles, or they will break up completely.

Glass Noodles

You might see these long, skinny noodles sold as bean-thread noodles or cellophane noodles. They are made of water and some type of starch—tapioca starch, mung bean starch, sweet potato starch, potato starch, or pea starch. Glass noodles are gluten-free, aren't as slurpy as the other noodles, and don't add much taste to the dish, but they do act as a flavor vehicle for the rest of the ingredients. If you're soaking them, try a tasty broth because the noodles absorb all that flavor.

Equipment

When I started making ramen, I used a hot plate, saucepan, and maybe chopsticks to stir everything up. So you don't need anything unusual to create most of the recipes in this book, but some require special items to produce similar results. A kitchen equipped with standard tools—the must-haves—is a decent place to start, and then add anything extra when you want to experiment. Nice-to-have equipment is used for a few of my recipes, so they are a good investment. Each piece of specialty equipment is used for one recipe but is fun for food other than ramen.

Here is the equipment to consider when tackling the recipes.

Must-Have Equipment

Bowls: You can never have too many bowls when experimenting. Stainless steel is a good choice for kitchen bowls because it doesn't rust and cleans up quickly. Pick up a set of nested bowls for easy storage.

Cookware: Saucepans and skillets are used for many ramen recipes, so grab an assortment with different wall heights and widths to make your life easier. Nonstick cookware is convenient but unnecessary. At a minimum, have a medium skillet and medium saucepan in your kitchen.

Cutting boards: Pick up some cutting boards in different sizes, and if possible, keep one exclusively for animal proteins to avoid contamination. For sanitation reasons, raw meat and fish should be cut on a plastic or other non-wood cutting board.

High-quality kitchen knives: You won't be preparing huge mounds of vegetables, but I like some in ramen to add texture, flavor, and a pop of color. A sharp, professional knife saves time and energy chopping, slicing, and mincing vegetables, fruit, and proteins. If you've never purchased a good knife, head to the store and hold a few; the one you pick should have a good weight and length and feel comfortable in your hand. I would get a 6-inch (15 cm) chef's knife and a paring knife to start.

Measuring cups and spoons: Accurate measurements, in most cases, ensure your recipes come out right. If possible, grab a complete set of wet and dry measuring cups as well as spoons ranging from 1 tablespoon to ⅛ teaspoon. If space or budget concerns you, have a 1-cup measure and a set of spoons.

Rapid ramen cooker: I use this for many recipes in this book, and it's so convenient. You just put the ramen noodles in, add liquid, and microwave it. The cooker cleans up quickly and can be used to reheat leftovers, too. If you don't have a rapid ramen cooker, microwave-safe bowls are a perfect substitute.

Spatula: This tool makes flipping proteins and sandwiches a snap. A silicone spatula is best because it's easy to clean, heat resistant, and stain resistant, and it won't scratch your nonstick cookware.

Nice-to-Have Equipment

Bullet-style blender: I use this for the purées I use to cook ramen noodles, like kiwi, watermelon, and, in one crazy late-night session, hamburgers. It's less expensive than a full-size blender or food processor, it's easy to clean, and it takes up little space in your kitchen.

Large stock pot: One of my Cooking with Friends guests showed me how to make excellent chicken stock for tasty ramen. We used a larger pot because lots of ingredients and water are needed for the best taste. A 12-quart (11 L) pot is a good size for most home cooks.

Microwave: I'm putting this appliance under nice to have because most ramen recipes can be done on a stovetop or hot plate. However, microwaves are essential for some of the dishes.

Baking dishes (9- and 8-inch/23 and 20 cm square): I use these to make my Ramen Lasagna (page 111) and a couple of other recipes in this book. You can use nonstick bakeware or glass—either will work.

Specialty Equipment

Air fryer: In this book, you will find french fries, nuggets, and pumpkin seeds cooked in an air fryer. It is a handy, versatile appliance, but you can also use a standard oven. If you decide to get an air fryer, you won't regret it.

Easter egg molds: I used this baking pan for my Ramen Deviled Eggs (page 150) because the molds were the perfect shape and size for what I needed.

Mini donut mold: I used this specialty mold for Ramen Onion Rings (page 143) to create the shape and ensure the rings were crispy on all sides. You could bake the rings in another container if this type of mold isn't available, like muffin tins.

Toaster bag: These washable bags can be used again and again—the manufacturers say about 100 times—if you follow the care instructions. That is a lot of Ramen Omelets (page 57), or grilled cheese sandwiches if you're not in the mood for ramen.

Waffle maker: Who doesn't love crispy golden waffles? This appliance lets you whip them up in minutes whenever the craving strikes. I use it for Fried Chicken and Waffles (page 40).

Frequently Used Ingredients

Besides ramen packages and noodle bundles, here are the most common ingredients you might need to make the recipes in this book. Obviously, you can throw anything in and create incredible versions of ramen on your own.

Proteins

- Bacon
- Beef (sirloin steak, shaved, stir-fry strips)
- Butter
- Cheese—shredded or sliced (cheddar, American, mozzarella)
- Chicken (boneless skinless breasts, wings)
- Deli meats
- Eggs
- Hot dogs
- Milk
- Seafood (salmon, shrimp, crab legs, octopus)
- Tofu

Vegetables and Fruits

- Apple
- Baby bok choy
- Carrot
- Celery
- Garlic cloves
- Jalapeño pepper
- Kiwi
- Lemon
- Mushrooms (shiitake, white, enoki, baby bella, cremini)
- Onion
- Pineapple
- Radish
- Red dragon fruit
- Scallion
- Swiss chard
- Tomato
- Zucchini

Condiments

- Buffalo hot sauce
- Chick-fil-A sauce
- Mayonnaise
- Mustard
- Sichuan chili sauce
- Soy sauce
- Sriracha sauce

Pantry

- Black pepper
- Honey
- Oils (olive oil, sesame oil, vegetable oil, oil spray)
- Rice
- Salt
- Spicy tortilla chips

Freezer

- Dumplings (chicken, kimchi, broccoli)
- Frozen mixed veggies
- Seafood

Playing with Your Food

Growing up, I was constantly told not to play with my food. And one of the fun things about being an adult is I can do whatever I want with my food. Even better, I've created a career by playing with my food. To me, this just means not following every rule and combining ingredients and cooking techniques that don't traditionally mesh. Fine-dining restaurants do a more controlled version of this and call it fusion cooking. If you think outside the box, throw in an ingredient, and the finished meal is a hard pass, you won't make the same choice next time. But I bet it was fun. Occasionally, inspiration will strike, and when the smoke clears (not literally, I hope), you will be looking at and enjoying a spectacular cooking success—something to serve to the special people in your life.

Through the videos, mishaps, wigs, Cooking with Friends, shopping, and planning involved in my videos—yes, I plan!—I've realized that delicious food doesn't have to be expensive or complicated, or take up half your day. Most of the time, you can create incredible, satisfying meals with items from your own cupboard in less than 30 minutes.

Let's cook some ramen!

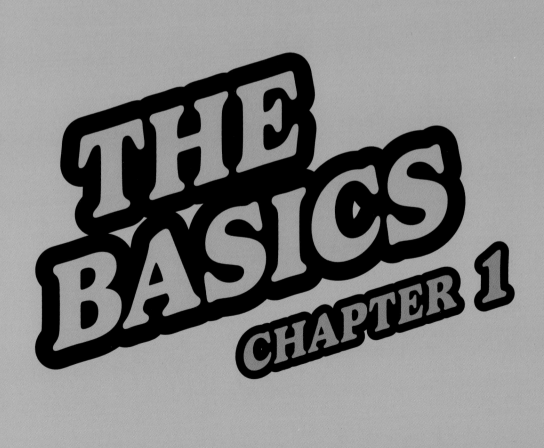

THE BASICS

CHAPTER 1

Original Ramen

2 cups (475 ml) water

1 package (3 ounces/85 g) instant ramen
noodles (any flavor)

You would be surprised how many times people have asked me how to make regular ramen! The possibilities are endless and up to your imagination, to be honest. But you can make it in the microwave, on the stovetop, or even in the oven! This is the simplest way possible.

1. In a small saucepan, bring the water to a boil over medium-high heat.

2. Add the ramen noodles.

3. Follow the package instructions for cook time (usually about 3 minutes), then remove the saucepan from the heat and stir in the seasoning packet.

4. Enjoy!

Soft-Boiled Egg

1 large egg

One question I'm constantly asked is how to make perfect soft-boiled eggs. Mine are so creamy and beautiful when sliced open and arranged on the ramen. Funnily enough, I was grossed out when I first saw a soft-boiled egg oozing everywhere, but it became a signature topping for my ramen. Heaven!

1. In a large saucepan, bring 4 cups (960 ml) of water to a rumbling boil.

2. Slowly lower the egg into the water using a spoon so it doesn't crack from hitting the bottom.

3. Boil the egg for 7 minutes (or 8 to 9 minutes for a harder yolk).

4. Transfer the egg to a bowl of ice water to stop the cooking process and let it sit for 1 to 2 minutes.

5. Crack and peel the egg.

6. Slice it down the middle and admire the beautiful, perfectly cooked center!

TIP:
You can store these in the fridge for about 2 days after cooking them.

MAKES 4

PREP TIME: 5 MINUTES,
PLUS OVERNIGHT MARINATING

COOK TIME: 7 MINUTES

Korean-Style Marinated Eggs

4 large eggs

½ cup (120 ml) soy sauce

½ cup (120 ml) water

2 garlic cloves, minced

1 jalapeño pepper, sliced, with seeds

4 small red chili peppers, sliced, with seeds

3 scallions, white parts only, roughly chopped

1 tablespoon (8 g) toasted black sesame seeds

Soft-boiled eggs are an obsession of mine and a signature of my ramen recipes; I want them to be perfect. But Korean marinated eggs are so freaking good and add a little bit of spice to your ramen, especially when sriracha just isn't spicy enough. You can also drizzle some of the marinade over your ramen as a finishing touch. Delicious!

1. In a medium saucepan, bring 2 to 3 inches (5 to 7.5 cm) of water—enough to cover the eggs—to a boil over medium-high heat.

2. One by one, slowly lower the eggs into the water using a spoon so they don't crack from hitting the bottom.

3. Boil the eggs for 7 minutes.

4. Transfer the eggs to a bowl of ice water to stop the cooking process and let them sit for 1 to 2 minutes.

5. In a medium bowl, combine the soy sauce, ½ cup (120 ml) water, garlic, jalapeño pepper, chili peppers, scallion, and sesame seeds. Stir until mixed.

6. Peel the cooled eggs and add them to the marinade, cover the bowl with plastic wrap, and marinate in the refrigerator overnight.

7. Store eggs in the refrigerator for up to 2 days.

Chicken Bone Broth

8 cups (1.9 L) water

Bones from 6 chicken drumsticks (use the chicken meat for another recipe)

5 or 6 stalks celery, roughly chopped, including greens

2 large carrots, roughly chopped

1 large onion, cut into large chunks

5 garlic cloves, smashed

1 teaspoon whole peppercorns

1 teaspoon sea salt

You can make bone broth using any type of bones, like beef, lamb, or turkey—not just the deboned drumsticks in this recipe. I usually get a rotisserie chicken every weekend, and I save the bones to make bone broth with for my ramen. Fun fact: adding a couple tablespoons of apple cider vinegar to the pot helps to pull out more nutrients from the bones! I love making my own broth; it's a lengthy process, but worth it because you can make it taste exactly how you want.

1. Pour the water into a large pot and add the chicken bones, celery, carrots, onion, garlic, peppercorns, and salt.

2. Bring to a boil over medium-high heat.

3. Reduce the heat to low, cover, and simmer for 6 hours.

4. Let the broth cool slightly, then strain into large mason jars and discard the solids.

5. Store the bone broth in the refrigerator for up to 5 days. You can also freeze the bone broth in plastic containers for up to 3 months.

TIP:
You can store broth as ice cubes for easy use! Pour the broth into ice cube trays, freeze, then pop the cubes into a freezer bag to store in the freezer. Then you can take out a small amount to use whenever you want. I like a lot of broth, so I usually use about 10 cubes at a time, but if you want less broth, use fewer cubes!

SERVES 1

PREP TIME: 5 MINUTES

COOK TIME: 3 MINUTES

My First Video Ramen

1 package (3 ounces/85 g) instant ramen noodles (any flavor)

3 American cheese slices, stacked and cut into chunks

Sriracha sauce, for drizzling

Mayonnaise, for garnish

Dried parsley, for garnish

This recipe isn't a basic, but it is the ramen I featured in the very first video on my account. The idea came from a prison cookbook I found somewhere, and it tastes interesting. If you're stuck somewhere between a rock and a hard place and you have nothing else to eat, this will be the best meal you ever had. You can substitute whatever you have in your fridge—different cheeses, condiments, seasonings. The finished ramen will still be satisfying.

1. Break the ramen noodles into a medium serving bowl.

2. Pour 2 cups (475 ml) hot water over the ramen noodles, cover, and let sit for 3 minutes to soften.

3. Add the cheese, a drizzle of sriracha sauce, mayonnaise, ramen seasoning mix, and parsley.

4. Stir to combine and serve.

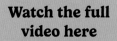

Watch the full video here

Insanely Good Ramen Meals

CHICKEN & TURKEY

CHAPTER 2

Chicken-Honey Ramen

1 package (3 ounces/85 g) ramen noodles (any flavor, but I prefer chicken)

2 teaspoons extra virgin olive oil

½ cup (125 g) shredded cooked chicken breast

1½ teaspoons to 1 tablespoon (10 to 20 g) honey

Salt, freshly ground black pepper, and any other seasonings you'd like, to taste

This recipe was inspired by a follower! They challenged me to make ramen with honey as the broth, because they thought there was no way honey would work. I accepted, flipped the concept, and made this masterpiece! It's really tasty, and worth the time.

1. Cook the ramen according to the package directions, including the seasoning packet.

2. While the ramen is cooking, heat the oil in a medium skillet over medium-high heat.

3. Add the chicken and sauté until lightly browned, about 2 to 3 minutes. Season as desired.

4. Top the ramen with the chicken and drizzle with the honey.

Fried Chicken and Waffles

SERVES 2
PREP TIME: 5 MINUTES
COOK TIME: 15 TO 20 MINUTES

2 packages (3 ounces/85 g each) instant ramen noodles (any flavor), divided

4 large eggs

2 (6-ounce) boneless, skinless chicken breasts, thinly sliced

3 cups (711 ml) vegetable oil

2½ cups (300 g) prepared waffle or pancake mix

Syrup, for serving

My mom used to take me to this diner when I was a kid, and I always got this comfort food dish. I decided to try to replicate the textures and taste with ramen and it worked better than I imagined. Who knew using ramen as breading is top notch and fun.

To Make the Fried Chicken

1. Crush one pack of ramen noodles, open it, and remove the seasoning packet.

2. Add the noodles to a blender with the seasoning and pulse until it is a flour-like consistency. Pour it into a medium bowl.

3. Whisk the eggs in another medium bowl and set them next to the "flour."

4. Dredge the chicken strips in the eggs and then the "flour" until well-breaded and set them aside on a plate.

5. Heat the oil in a large skillet over medium-high heat.

6. Working in batches, place the breaded chicken into the oil and cook, turning once, until completely cooked through and golden, about 6 to 8 minutes in total.

7. Transfer the chicken to a napkin-lined plate to soak up the excess oil and repeat until all the strips are cooked.

To Make the Waffles

1. Crush the remaining ramen packet and set aside the seasoning packet.

2. Add half of the ramen block, crushed into the pancake mix and cook according to the waffle/pancake mix instructions.

3. Top each waffle with crispy golden chicken strips and syrup.

NOTE:
To see if the oil is hot enough, dip a wooden spoon in it. If there are no bubbles around the spoon, it's not hot enough. If you see some bubbles, you are good to go!

Insanely Good Ramen Meals

SERVES 2

PREP TIME: 15 MINUTES

COOK TIME: 24 MINUTES

Ramen Chicken Nuggets

2 packages (3 ounces/85 g each) instant ramen noodles, chicken flavor

2 large eggs

1 (1-pound/455 g) package chicken tenders, cut into 1½-inch (3.8 cm) chunks

Sriracha sauce

Do you like ramen? Do you like chicken nuggets? Have you ever wanted to mix those two together to make the perfect meal? Me too! Ha! Ha! That is the reason I picked the suggestion from a follower to make this recipe. It's very simple and tastes great with any condiment.

1. Place one of the ramen noodle blocks and one of the seasoning packets in a blender and pulse until it is a fine flour consistency. Transfer the "flour" to a plate.

2. Crush the other noodle block in its bag and transfer to a plate.

3. Beat the eggs well in a small bowl.

4. Dredge the chicken chunks in the ramen flour, then the egg, then the crushed ramen.

5. Working in batches, fry the nuggets in an air fryer for 12 minutes at 350°F (180°C) or place about ¼-inch (6 mm) vegetable oil in a medium frying pan and cook nuggets for 5 minutes on each side, or until brown. Repeat until all the nuggets are cooked.

6. Serve with sriracha sauce.

Chicken Meatballs and Grape Ramen

1 tablespoon (15 ml) olive oil

1 package (12-ounce/340 g) fully cooked
chicken meatballs

2 cups (475 ml) whole milk

1 (125 g) bundle sōmen noodles

1½ cups (210 g) shredded mozzarella
cheese

1 grape-flavored Pixy Stix tube

The addition of grape in this dish was mostly for the purplish color, and honestly, you could use a couple drops of food coloring instead of Pixy Stix to create the same look. I used more shredded cheese in my video, so add a bit more if you want a super cheesy result. Any meatballs can be substituted, but the chicken ones add a nice look to the finished ramen.

1. Heat the olive oil in a medium skillet over medium-high heat.

2. Add the meatballs and warm, turning, until lightly browned all over and heated through, about 6 minutes. Transfer them to a plate and cover loosely with foil to keep them warm.

3. Add the milk to the same skillet and bring to a simmer.

4. Add the sōmen noodles and cook them according to the package directions.

5. Stir in the cheese until melted and gooey.

6. Stir in the grape flavoring.

7. Transfer the cheesy noodles to a serving bowl and top with the meatballs.

Chicken Dumpling and Watermelon Ramen

1 small seedless watermelon

1 (500 ml) bottle watermelon-flavored water, such as blk. brand

Salt

Freshly ground black pepper

1 tablespoon (15 ml) olive oil

1 tablespoon (15 ml) dark soy sauce

1 (125 g) bundle sōmen noodles

1 package (6.5-ounce/180 g) chicken dumplings

1 Soft-Boiled Egg (page 29), peeled and halved

Making a bowl out of a melon is fun, and half is left over for dessert or snacks, which is a win. The blk. water puréed with the watermelon adds an extra hint of flavor, but plain water won't change the taste very much. You will find that the salty soy sauce somehow makes the melon seem even sweeter. The chicken dumplings complement the rest of the ingredients, but any kind would be delicious.

1. Halve the watermelon. You'll only be using one half—save the other for snacking.

2. Scoop out four balls of melon using a melon baller or spoon and set aside. Scoop out the remaining flesh to create a bowl, transferring the contents into a blender.

3. Add half the flavored water to the blender and blend until smooth.

4. Pour the melon mixture into a medium skillet and season with salt and pepper. Bring to a simmer over medium-high heat.

5. Stir in the olive oil and soy sauce.

6. Add the sōmen noodles and cook them according to the package directions.

7. Place three of the reserved watermelon balls in the bottom of the rind bowl and add the noodles and sauce.

8. Prepare the dumplings according to the package directions and arrange them around the edges of the bowl.

9. Top with the egg and the last melon ball.

Pesto Chicken Ramen

1 teaspoon olive oil

1 package (6-ounce/170 g) pesto-flavored chicken breast, such as Trader Joe's

1 package (3 ounces/85 g) instant ramen noodles, chicken flavor

2 scallions, white and green parts, chopped

1 Soft-Boiled Egg (page 29), peeled and halved

Sriracha sauce, for drizzling

Chicken ramen is one of my favorites. Topping your meal with chicken adds extra flavor and protein, and it is delicious. I like a seasoned, marinated product because it saves time, or even rotisserie chicken. But you can use any type of chicken you have on hand and whatever sauce, spice, or herb that suits your palate. Ramen is a flexible ingredient; it goes with everything.

1. Heat the oil in a small skillet over medium-high heat and cook the chicken, turning once, until cooked through, about 8 minutes total. Slice the cooked chicken.

2. Place the ramen noodles in a microwave-safe bowl or rapid ramen cooker with ½ cup (120 ml) of water and microwave for 3 minutes.

3. Add the seasoning packet, stirring to combine.

4. Transfer the ramen and liquid to a serving bowl and arrange the chicken on top.

5. Garnish with scallions, the egg, and a drizzle of sriracha.

Ramen Buffalo Chicken Wings

1 cup (26 g) crushed, spicy tortilla chips, such as Paqui or Doritos

2 large eggs

½ cup (60 g) flour

1 package (3 ounces/85 g) instant ramen noodles, chicken flavor

1 pound (455 g) whole chicken wings

Olive oil, for frying

½ cup (120 ml) buffalo hot sauce

I'm a big fan of chicken wings, especially around sports season, but I like my chicken wings extra crunchy and extra crispy with a little extra spice! A follower asked me to make chicken wings, and because I'm the Ramen King, of course, they wanted added ramen. This recipe will also work with drumettes or flats, rather than the entire chicken wing. If you don't like spice, feel free to use other sauces, like honey, garlic, or lemon pepper.

1. Place the crushed spicy tortilla chips, eggs, and flour in three separate medium bowls. Beat the eggs until frothy.

2. Crush the ramen noodles in the bag and save the seasoning packet for another recipe.

3. Dredge the wings in the flour, then egg, then crushed spicy tortilla chips until coated but still wet.

4. Sprinkle the crushed ramen over the wings.

5. Pour 2 to 3 inches (5 to 7.5 cm) of oil in a large saucepan and heat to 350°F (180°C) over medium heat.

6. Working in batches, fry the wings, turning once, until golden and cooked through, about 10 to 12 minutes. Repeat until all the wings are cooked.

7. Transfer the wings to a large bowl and add the buffalo hot sauce, toss until coated.

Ginger-Lemon Soda Chicken Ramen

2 6-ounce (170 g) boneless, skinless chicken breasts

Salt

Pepper

1 teaspoon ginger paste or finely minced ginger

1 12-ounce (355 ml) can ginger-lemon soda

1 tablespoon (15 ml) olive oil

8 to 10 cremini mushrooms, sliced

3 packages (3 ounces/85 g each) instant ramen noodles, chicken flavor

Sriracha sauce

3 Soft-Boiled Eggs (page 29), peeled and halved

I created this recipe for a brand by the name of Ollipop! They wanted me to use their soda so I figured, *Why not? I can make some chicken with that combo!* After all, both ginger and lemon are used across many of the world's cuisines to enhance chicken. So glad I took on the challenge—it came out nicely!

1. Place the chicken in medium bowl, season to taste with salt, pepper, and ginger, then pour in the soda.

2. Marinate the chicken in the refrigerator for 20 minutes.

3. Heat the oil in a small skillet over medium-high heat and sauté the mushrooms until golden, about 3 minutes. Remove with a slotted spoon to a bowl and set aside.

4. Place the ramen noodles in a large casserole dish, add enough boiling water to cover them, cover the dish, and set it aside until the noodles are softened, about 3 to 5 minutes.

5. While the noodles are soaking, pan-fry the chicken in the same skillet as the mushrooms until cooked through and golden, turning once, about 12 minutes total.

6. Slice the chicken and set aside.

7. Add the seasoning packets, a squeeze of sriracha, and a drizzle of water to the ramen. Stir to combine.

8. Divide the ramen between two bowls. Arrange the sautéed mushrooms on one side of the ramen and the chicken on the other.

9. Top with the eggs and a drizzle of sriracha.

Ramen Breakfast Burrito

SERVES 1

PREP TIME: 5 MINUTES

COOK TIME: 10 TO 15 MINUTES

1 package (3 ounces/85 g) instant ramen noodles, chicken flavor

1 tablespoon (14 g) butter

3 slices bacon (turkey or pork)

"Everything bagel" seasoning

4 slices cheddar

4 large eggs, beaten

1 9-inch (23 cm) flour tortilla

Salt

Freshly ground black pepper

If you put *anything* inside of a burrito, I'll eat it! I wanted to test that theory with breakfast—and ramen—so I created this amazing burrito. Feel free to swap out some of the ingredients for veggies, cooked sausage meat, and other cheeses. If meal prep is your thing, make two burritos, halve them, pop each half into a sealable plastic bag, and store in the refrigerator for up to five days.

1. Put the ramen noodles in a medium bowl and cover them with hot water. Let sit for 3 minutes to soften, then strain out the water. Save the seasoning packet for another recipe.

2. Melt the butter in a large skillet over medium heat.

3. Cook the bacon, turning once, until crispy, about 5 minutes total.

4. Spread the ramen noodles over the bacon and sprinkle with bagel seasoning.

5. Cover with the cheese slices, pour in the egg, and top with the tortilla. Cook until the egg is set, about 2 to 3 minutes.

6. Turn the tortilla out onto a cutting board, filling side up, and season with salt and pepper.

7. Roll the tortilla into a cylinder, cut in half width-wise, and enjoy!

Ramen Omelet with Turkey Bacon

1 package (3 ounces/85 g) instant ramen noodles, chicken flavor

2 large eggs, beaten

1 slice turkey bacon, chopped

1 medium cremini mushroom, chopped

2 tablespoons (15 g) shredded Mexican-style cheese

I created this recipe for a toaster bag brand. You put anything inside the bag and pop it into your toaster—it's heatproof and reusable. Pretty cool! I put the bag to the test, making a ramen omelet and thought it might not work very well, but to my surprise it did! If you can't find toaster bags, just pour your ingredients into a skillet and make the omelet the old-fashioned way.

1. Crush the ramen noodles and place them in a small bowl.

2. Add the eggs, bacon, mushroom, cheese, and seasoning packet to the noodles and stir to combine.

3. Pour the egg mixture into a toaster bag and toast until cooked through, about 4 minutes, or cook in a buttered skillet.

Ramen Turkey Chili

1 3-ounce (85 g) package instant ramen noodles, chili flavor

1 12-ounce (340 g) package turkey Bolognese, like Trader Joe's Just Sauce

1 scallion, white and green parts, chopped

1 Soft-Boiled Egg (page 29), peeled and halved

This dish is another early-morning inspiration—I really need to work on my sleep! Like many other recipes, you can play around with the ingredients; there are no wrong choices if it tastes good in the end. If time isn't an issue, throw in some canned beans with sautéed onion and bell pepper to ramp up the chili experience.

1. Place the ramen noodles in a microwave-safe bowl or rapid ramen cooker with ½ cup (120 ml) of water and microwave for 3 minutes. Stir to break up the noodles and pour the noodles and liquid into a serving bowl.

2. Prepare the turkey Bolognese sauce according to the package directions and pour it into the ramen, stirring to combine.

3. Top with the scallions and egg.

BEEF

CHAPTER 3

Wagyu Beef Ramen

Oil spray

½ pound (225 g) sirloin beef stir-fry strips

2 cups (475 ml) blk. water

1 package (3 ounces/85 g) instant ramen noodles, beef flavor

2 scallions, white and green parts, chopped

¼ teaspoon "everything bagel" seasoning blend

1 Soft-Boiled Egg (page 29), peeled and halved

First off, you do not have to use blk. water for this recipe. Blk. water is just regular water with added minerals that turn the water black—it looks cool on camera, but it does not affect the taste of the food. If you want to make a cool-looking dish, go pick up a bottle.

1. Heat a medium skillet over medium-high heat and spray with oil. Sauté the beef until medium, about 2 to 3 minutes.

2. Remove the skillet from the heat and set it aside.

3. In a medium saucepan, heat 2 cups (475 ml) of water until simmering, then add the ramen noodles. Cook for exactly 3 minutes, then pour ramen and liquid into a serving bowl.

4. Top the ramen with the beef and scallions.

5. Sprinkle with the beef seasoning packet and everything bagel seasoning blend, then add the egg.

SERVES 1
PREP TIME: 10 MINUTES
COOK TIME: 20 MINUTES

Beef Naruto Ramen

2 cups (475 ml) water, divided

1 beef ramen seasoning packet

1 package (3 ounces/85 g) instant ramen noodles (any flavor)

3 scallions, chopped, with white bulbs reserved

1 8-ounce (225 g) top sirloin steak

1 tablespoon (14 g) butter

2 Soft-Boiled Eggs (page 29), peeled and halved

Naruto is one of my favorite anime series. I relate to Naruto's stories so much—being an underdog and rising to success by hard work and determination! He is known for eating a bunch of ramen so, of course, everyone always asks me to make ramen inspired by Naruto! This is my interpretation of the meal, since naruto (or nauromaki) is also a type of garnish commonly used on ramen.

1. Pour half the water into a medium saucepan and add both seasoning packets. Bring the water to a simmer over medium heat.

2. Pour the remaining water into a small saucepan and bring to a simmer over medium heat.

3. Place the scallion bulbs and chopped green parts in the water with the seasoning.

4. In a medium skillet over high heat, sear the steak, turning once, until medium rare, about 8 minutes total.

5. Remove the skillet from the heat, top the steak with the butter, and set it aside.

6. Place the ramen noodles in the second saucepan and simmer until softened, about 3 minutes.

7. Pour the ramen noodles and liquid into a serving bowl. Pour all the scallion broth over the noodles, arranging the bulbs and chopped greens evenly.

8. Arrange the eggs on the edge of the bowl.

9. Thinly slice the steak on the bias and arrange the meat on the ramen.

Big M Ramen

1 Big Mac

1 small McDonald's fries

½ cup (120 ml) water

1 package (3 ounces/85 g) instant ramen noodles (any flavor)

Oil spray

½ cup (35 g) sliced white mushrooms

1 Soft-Boiled Egg (page 29), peeled and halved

Heinz Honeyracha sauce, for drizzling

Fair warning: this may not be 1,000 percent amazing to everyone's taste, but it's a fun recipe to try! I was challenged to turn a Big Mac meal into a ramen dish. The Honeyracha made it taste better, but that sauce may not be available everywhere. It's basically just honey mixed with sriracha, so you can make it at home. This recipe calls for reserving some broth with the ramen noodles, but you don't have to do that if you prefer it on the drier side.

1. Place the Big Mac, fries, and water in a blender and pulse until it is a smooth liquid.

2. Pour the liquid into a small saucepan and bring to a simmer over medium heat.

3. While the sauce is heating up, place the ramen noodles in a microwave-safe bowl or instant ramen cooker with ½ cup (120 ml) of water and microwave for 3 minutes.

4. Place a small skillet over medium heat and spray with oil. Sauté the mushrooms until browned, about 2 minutes.

5. Drain some liquid from the noodles, reserving some of the broth with the noodles.

6. Place the cooked ramen and remaining broth on a serving bowl. Top with the mushrooms and spoon the sauce over the noodles.

7. Top with the egg and a drizzle of Honeyracha sauce. Enjoy!

Jerky and Bok Choy Ramen

1 tablespoon (15 ml) olive oil

1 large baby bok choy, base removed

3 scallions, white and green parts, chopped

1 1-ounce (32 g) stick beef jerky, chopped

1 tablespoon (15 ml) toasted sesame oil

1 package (3 ounces/85 g) instant ramen noodles, beef flavor

1 Soft-Boiled Egg (page 29), peeled and halved

Sriracha sauce, for drizzling

Jerky is dehydrated meat. All the flavor is condensed, so when it's rehydrated, that flavor is released into the water. This is the thought process going through my mind when I purchased a bunch of jerky. I was right! This recipe is amazing—absolutely delicious.

1. Heat the olive oil in a small skillet over medium heat. Add the bok choy, scallions, and jerky and sauté until the veggies are tender, about 5 minutes.

2. Drizzle in the sesame oil and cook for 1 minute. Remove the skillet from the heat and set it aside.

3. Bring 2 cups (475 ml) of water to a boil in a small saucepan over medium heat.

4. Add the ramen and boil for 3 minutes, drain half the water, and stir in the seasoning packet.

5. Pour the ramen into a serving bowl and add the jerky/veggie mixture.

6. Top with the egg and a drizzle of sriracha.

Deli Meat Ramen Sandwich

SERVES 1
PREP TIME: 5 MINUTES, PLUS 5
MINUTES SOAKING TIME
COOK TIME: 15 TO 20 MINUTES

1 package (3 ounces/85 g) instant ramen noodles (any flavor)

2 tablespoons (28 g) butter

Mustard

Mayonnaise

Deli meat, such as roast beef or ham (your choice)

1 slice of cheese (your choice)

1 scallion, thinly sliced

1 Soft-Boiled Egg (page 29)

This recipe started out as a science experiment! I wondered what ramen would taste like as a sandwich . . . I honestly didn't think it would work, but here we are, and it's pretty good—especially if you're out of bread. The lesson learned is play with your food!

1. Remove the noodles from the packaging and separate the block into two pieces of "bread." Place them on a plate big enough to hold both and with a bit of a slope/lip. Save the seasoning packets for another recipe.

2. Pour enough hot water onto the plate to cover the ramen halfway. Be careful not to use too much; you want some of the noodles hard, so it holds together!

3. Let the ramen sit for 5 minutes or until it is soft to the touch.

4. Melt the butter in a skillet over low to medium heat.

5. Place one ramen piece in the skillet, soft side down, and brown, cooking about 2 to 3 minutes. Transfer the piece to a plate and repeat with the other piece of "bread."

6. Layer the sandwich ingredients on one of the "bread" pieces, starting with a slather of mustard and mayo. Feel free to work outside the box with your own combination of ingredients.

7. Slice your perfect soft-boiled egg and drizzle the yolk over the sandwich.

8. Slice the egg whites onto the sandwich and top the sandwich with the remaining "bread" slice.

BEEF   71

Stir-Fry Shaved Beef Ramen

2 teaspoons olive oil

½ pound (225 g) shaved beef

Salt

Freshly ground black pepper

Liquid smoke

4 scallions, white and green parts, chopped

1 (2¾-ounce/78 g) Cup Noodles Stir Fry Rice with Noodles, Korean spicy beef flavor

1 package (180 g) chicken dumplings

3 soft-boiled quail eggs or 1 Soft-Boiled Egg (page 29), peeled and halved

Sriracha sauce, for drizzling

I was experimenting with Cup Noodles and wanted to do a stir-fry meal with whatever I had in the fridge. I seem to do that a lot! You can scale up this recipe easily if you have people to feed, but when making multiple portions, chicken eggs are the way to go. Quail eggs cook quickly—about 2 minutes to soft boil—but can be tricky to peel because they are so small. Try this dish with chicken, different vegetables, and plain rice for different variations. Keep the smoky seasoning, if possible, even using liquid smoke to mimic a grilled taste.

1. Heat the oil in a medium skillet over medium-high heat. Add the beef and sauté until it is cooked through, about 5 minutes.

2. Season the meat with salt, pepper, and the smoke seasoning blend.

3. Add the scallions and sauté until bright green and tender, about 2 minutes.

4. Prepare the Cup Noodles according to the package directions.

5. Prepare the dumplings according to the package directions.

6. Arrange the beef scallion mixture around the edges of a medium serving bowl and add the noodles and rice in the center. Place the dumplings along one side of the bowl.

7. Top with the egg(s) and a drizzle of sriracha sauce.

SERVES 1

PREP TIME: 10 MINUTES

COOK TIME: 15 MINUTES

Blood on the Floor

1 (500 ml) bottle dark berry-flavored water, such as blk. brand Black and Blueberry flavor

1 (125 g) container blueberries

1 (125 g) container blackberries

1 tablespoon (15 ml) olive oil

1 tablespoon (15 ml) dark soy sauce

Salt

Freshly ground black pepper

1 (125 g) bundle sōmen noodles

1 package (16-ounce/455 g) Trader Joe's Beef Birria or other Mexican-flavored beef, such as carne asada

1 package (8.8-ounce/250 g) microwavable rice, roasted chicken flavor

1 Soft-Boiled Egg (page 29), peeled and halved

Hot sauce, such as Tabasco, for drizzling

Sometimes I use fruit to change the color of the broth, in this case blueberries and blackberries. The liquid doesn't have to be blk. water; you can use plain water. Most of my recipes are about playing with your food, but there isn't a single ingredient in this one I would change (besides the water!). Fruit is a nice combination with the beef—It's like drinking red wine while eating a juicy steak.

1. Combine the water, blueberries, and blackberries in a blender and blend until smooth.

2. Pour the mixture into a medium saucepan over medium-high heat.

3. Stir in the olive oil and soy sauce and season with salt and pepper.

4. Add the sōmen noodles and cook them according to the package directions.

5. Prepare the beef birria and rice according to the package directions.

6. Pour the hot rice into the center of a medium serving bowl and top with the sōmen noodles and beef birria (including the sauce).

7. Garnish with the egg and a drizzle of hot sauce.

SERVES 1
PREP TIME: 10 MINUTES
COOK TIME: 7 MINUTES

Zesty Ramen

1 tablespoon (15 ml) olive oil

1 package (12-ounce/350 g) dumplings, such as Sajo Vegan 0.6 Dumplings

1 (125 g) bundle sōmen noodles

1 packet (5-ounce/140 g) Korean-style spicy stew mix, such as CJ Dadam Spicy Stew Stock

1 tablespoon (6 g) puréed fresh ginger

1 lemon, halved width-wise

Leftover lemons inspired this dish. I used the rinds as taco shells, which people loved because it was unusual. This ramen recipe needed a little extra oomph, and citrus seemed like a perfect choice. I keep the rind on for that extra crunch, but feel free to remove it if you don't like that—just be sure to add a generous squeeze of juice and a bit of zest instead.

1. Heat the olive oil in a medium skillet over medium-high heat. Add the dumplings and cook them until lightly browned according to the package directions, about 4 minutes. Remove the skillet from the heat.

2. Bring 2 cups (475 ml) of water to a boil in a small saucepan over medium-high heat. Add the sōmen noodles and cook them according to the package directions.

3. While the noodles are cooking, place a medium skillet over medium-high heat and add the spicy stew stock and ginger, stirring to combine.

4. Slice one lemon half into ¼-inch (6 mm) rounds, quarter the rounds, and add them to the spicy ginger sauce. Heat until just simmering, about 3 minutes.

5. Drain and transfer the noodles to a medium serving bowl. Top with the sauce.

6. Slice the remaining lemon half into ¼-inch (6 mm) rounds and arrange them on one side of the bowl.

7. Arrange the cooked dumplings on the other side of the bowl and top them with a little of the sauce.

Beef Ramen

1 package (3 ounces/85 g) instant ramen noodles, beef flavor

1 package (16-ounce/455 g) Trader Joe's Beef Birria, or other Mexican-flavored beef, such as carne asada

1 Soft-Boiled Egg (page 29), peeled and halved

6-inch (15 cm) soft tortillas (optional)

The video for this recipe made people mad because I insulted cheap ramen by saying this preparation was my favorite. I know instant ramen is supposed to be cheap, but you can boost it up a little bit. In this case, adding meat just takes it up another notch. I used a Trader Joe's product, but ground beef, sliced steak, or even leftover beef stew would be cool.

1. Place the ramen noodles in a microwave-safe bowl or rapid ramen cooker with ½ cup (120 ml) of water and microwave for 3 minutes.

2. Prepare the beef birria according to the package directions.

3. Pour half the packaged beef sauce into the cooked ramen noodles and stir to combine.

4. Add the beef chunks and the halved egg, drizzling some sauce on the egg.

5. Eat as is or arrange the noodles, beef chunks, and egg in the center of the tortillas and fold them over to create tacos.

6. Pour the leftover beef sauce into a small bowl and use it as a dip for the tacos.

Ramen Beef Burrito

2 tablespoons (30 ml) olive oil

1 pound (455 g) lean ground beef

3 packages (3 ounces/85 g each) instant ramen noodles, chili flavor

6 8-inch (20 cm) flour tortillas

1 jar (15.5-ounce/460 ml) guacamole, such as Kroger Medium Guacamole Salsa

1 package (11.25-ounce/320 g) Mexican-style cheese

As I said earlier, if you put anything into a burrito, I will eat it. The question is, how much can be stuffed into a burrito before it busts apart? This recipe is my attempt to find out . . . using six overlapping tortillas to create a huge burrito base. Jazz up your burrito with favorite toppings like tomato salsa, jalapeño peppers, chicken instead of beef, or queso sauce instead of shredded cheese. Yum!

1. Heat the oil in a medium skillet over medium-high heat and brown the ground beef, about 8 minutes. Drain the oil and set the meat aside.

2. While the beef is cooking, working in batches, place the ramen noodles in a microwave-safe bowl or rapid ramen cooker with ½ cup (120 ml) of water and microwave each for 3 minutes. Stir to break up the noodles and pour the noodles into a serving bowl.

3. Layer the tortillas, overlapping each by about one-third, to create one large work surface.

4. Spread the guacamole all over the tortillas, leaving about 1 inch (2.5 cm) around the edge.

5. Sprinkle half the cheese over the guacamole and spread the cooked beef over the cheese.

6. Arrange the cooked ramen noodles down the center and sprinkle with 2 of the seasoning packets. Top with the remaining cheese and use a kitchen torch to melt it. If you don't own a torch, put the whole thing in the oven on broil for about 5 minutes, or until melted (just make sure your serving bowl is oven-safe).

7. Fold the sides of the burrito into the center and roll the burrito toward you to create a sealed package.

8. Cut it in half and enjoy with a ton of napkins!

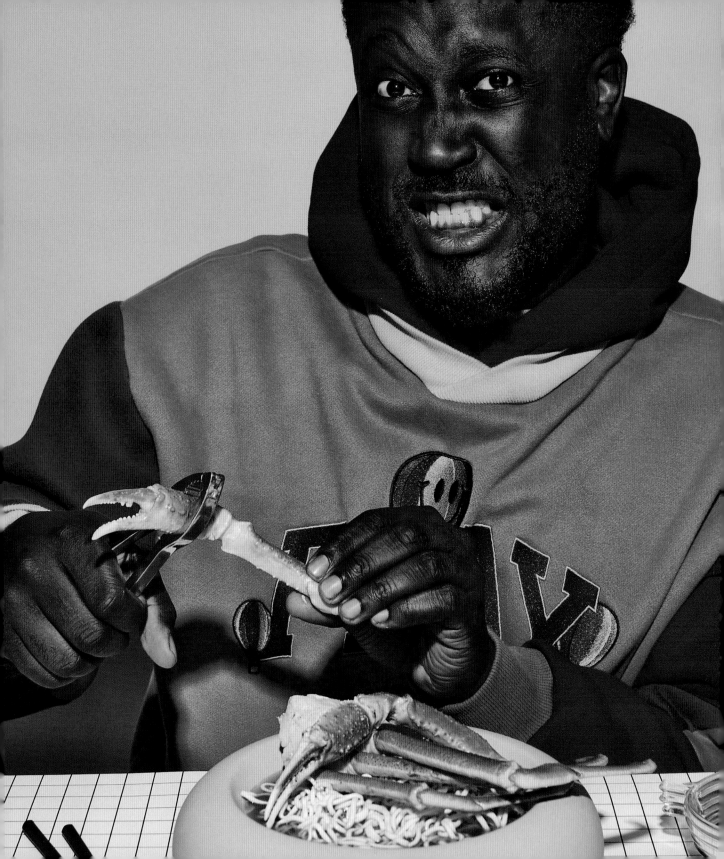

SEAFOOD
CHAPTER 4

Tilapia Ramen

1 tablespoon (15 ml) olive oil

8-ounce (225 g) tilapia fillet, cut into
2-inch (5-cm) chunks

1 chicken ramen seasoning packet

1 package (6.21-ounce/176 g) ramen,
tonkotsu pork flavor (such as Kumamoto)

2 Soft-Boiled Eggs (page 29), peeled and
halved

2 scallions, white and green parts,
chopped

Thai chili sriracha, for drizzling

I had never cooked tilapia before this recipe, and now it is my first choice of fish, tied with salmon. A video of someone else meal prepping with it gave me the idea to use it in ramen. You could serve this dish to guests and be proud—it looks and tastes amazing, and it is very simple to make.

1. Heat the oil in a large skillet over medium-high heat and add the tilapia. Sprinkle the fish with the seasoning and cook, turning once, until lightly browned and just cooked through, about 8 minutes total.

2. Bring 2 cups (475 ml) of water to a boil in a medium saucepan over medium-high heat. Add the noodles and cook them according to the package directions.

3. Transfer the noodles and cooking liquid to a serving bowl and stir in the seasoning and sauce packets.

4. Top the noodles with the fish, the eggs, the scallions, and a drizzle of sriracha.

Ramen Sardine Surprise

1 package (3 ounces/85 g) instant ramen noodles, chicken flavor

2 tablespoons (28 g) mayonnaise

1 tablespoon (11 g) mustard

1 can (3.7-ounce/105 g) smoked sardines in oil

2 smoked turkey jerky sticks, chopped

Sriracha sauce, for drizzling

If you have a can of smoked sardines in your cupboard and you're just plain hungry, throw this meal together quick. It's fun to make and can be a spectacular spread on crackers or a dip if you mix it up well. Salty, smoky, creamy, and a bit of heat—what could be better than that in a pinch?

1. Place the ramen noodles in a microwave-safe bowls or rapid ramen cooker with ½ cup (120 ml) of water and microwave each for 3 minutes. Stir to break up the noodles and drain. Save the seasoning packets for another recipe.

2. Stir in the mayonnaise and mustard.

3. Add the sardines in oil and the turkey sausage. Stir to combine and top with sriracha.

Shrimp Rice Cake Ramen

1 (290 g) package tteokbokki Korean rice cakes with sweet chili sauce

1 tablespoon (15 ml) olive oil

1 package (16-ounce/455 g) shrimp (21- to 30-count), peeled, deveined, tail on

Salt

Pepper

2 (125 g) bundles sōmen noodles

2 Soft-Boiled Eggs (page 29), peeled and halved

Maria Legarda from my Cooking with Friends series dropped in just as I was starting this recipe, so she stayed to help with it. Her very hands-on cooking technique included flipping the sautéing shrimp with her fingers, but you should use tongs or just turn them with a spoon. Look for Korean rice cakes in East Asian food stores or the international food section of your supermarket. They are perfect with any ramen dish.

1. Pour the rice cakes into a large skillet and add enough water to cover them by 1 inch (2.5 cm). Soak the rice cakes for 4 to 5 minutes, then drain.

2. While the rice cakes are soaking, heat the oil in a large skillet over medium-high heat and add the shrimp. Season with salt and pepper and sauté until opaque and cooked through, about 6 minutes.

3. Add 1 cup (235 ml) of fresh water to the skillet with the rice cakes and bring to a simmer on medium-high heat.

4. Bring 2 cups (475 ml) of water to a boil in a small saucepan over medium-high heat. Add the sōmen noodles and cook them according to the package directions.

5. Add the cooked shrimp to the skillet with the rice cakes, stirring to combine.

6. Evenly divide the cooked noodles between 2 serving bowls and top each with the shrimp rice cake mixture and a generous ladle of the sweet chili sauce.

7. Garnish with the eggs and a drizzle of the sauce.

Mako Shark Jerky Ramen

SERVES 1
PREP TIME: 10 MINUTES
COOK TIME: 10 MINUTES

1 package (3-ounce/85 g) mako shark jerky

Salt

7 or 8 shiitake mushrooms, sliced

1 package (3 ounces/85 g) instant ramen noodles, chicken flavor

1 large egg yolk

1 scallion, white and green parts, chopped

Sriracha sauce, for drizzling

Farmers' markets have incredible products. I come home with something delicious every time I go, like this mako jerky. It was gamey, not fishy, and since Jerky and Bok Choy Ramen (page 69) turned out well, I thought, *Why not?* When you heat up any kind of jerky in water, it rehydrates the meat and releases all that flavor into the liquid, creating a tasty broth. I would have added more jerky to the water to intensify the flavor, but I only had a small bag—you do what tastes right to you!

1. Pour 2 cups (475 ml) of water into a medium saucepan, add the jerky, and season lightly with salt. Bring the water to a simmer over medium-high heat.

2. Add the mushrooms, the ramen noodles, and three-quarters of the ramen seasoning packet. Cover and simmer for 2 to 3 minutes, until the noodles and mushrooms are tender.

3. Add the egg yolk and stir for 1 minute to combine.

4. Arrange the noodles in the center of a serving bowl and ladle the broth, mushrooms, and mako shark on top of the noodles.

5. Garnish with the scallions and a drizzle of sriracha.

$15 Budget Salmon Meal

1 tablespoon (15 ml) olive oil

1 6-ounce (170 g) skin-on salmon fillet

2 (76 g) instant ramen, curry flavor, such as Cup Noodles Stir Fry Rice with Noodles Thai yellow curry flavor

1 package (10.8-ounce/306 g) frozen vegetable mix, such as Birds Eye Asian Medley

1 Soft-Boiled Egg (page 29), peeled and halved

Sriracha sauce, for drizzling

Another challenge: could I make a delicious, filling meal for only $15? The answer is yes, and this recipe is amazing! I've made it again for friends, spending even less per person by shopping around. You can use any type of frozen vegetable, but East Asian–style mixes seem to combine perfectly with the other ingredients.

1. Heat the olive oil in a small skillet over medium-high heat.

2. While the oil is warming up, season the salmon with the seasoning from the first package of ramen, patting the mixture all over the top of the fish. Set the noodles aside for another use.

3. Cook the fish skin side down until lightly browned, about 4 minutes.

4. Flip the fish with a spatula and cook until it is cooked through, about 3 minutes.

5. Prepare the second package of ramen according to the instructions and pour it into a medium serving bowl.

6. Prepare the vegetables according to the package directions and pour them into the serving bowl.

7. Remove the skin from the salmon and chop the fish, arranging it on the vegetables.

8. Garnish with the egg and a drizzle of sriracha and serve.

Seafood Ramen

1 (360 g) package stir fry short arm octopus kit, I use Hwawoodang brand

1 (125 g) bundle sōmen noodles

1 Soft-Boiled Egg (page 29), peeled and halved

Sriracha sauce, for drizzling

The original plan for this dish was to use a whole octopus, but as I stood in front of the seafood counter, it hit me: I don't know how to cook an octopus. And wouldn't there be a ton of leftover tentacles and stuff that I'd be eating for days? Then I saw a kit in the frozen food section, and it looked easy, interesting, and seafoody. It was a very good choice—the octopus was tender and perfectly seasoned, and it absorbed all the juices and spicy sauce. Any kit like this would work in this dish.

1. Remove the contents from the kit packaging and transfer them to a medium skillet over medium-high heat. Pan-fry according to the package directions until the octopus is fully cooked.

2. Heat 2 cups (475 ml) of water in a medium saucepan over medium-high heat. Add the sōmen noodles and cook them according to the directions.

3. Drain the noodles and add them to the octopus mixture, stirring to combine.

4. Transfer the ramen to a medium serving bowl, top with the egg, and drizzle with sriracha.

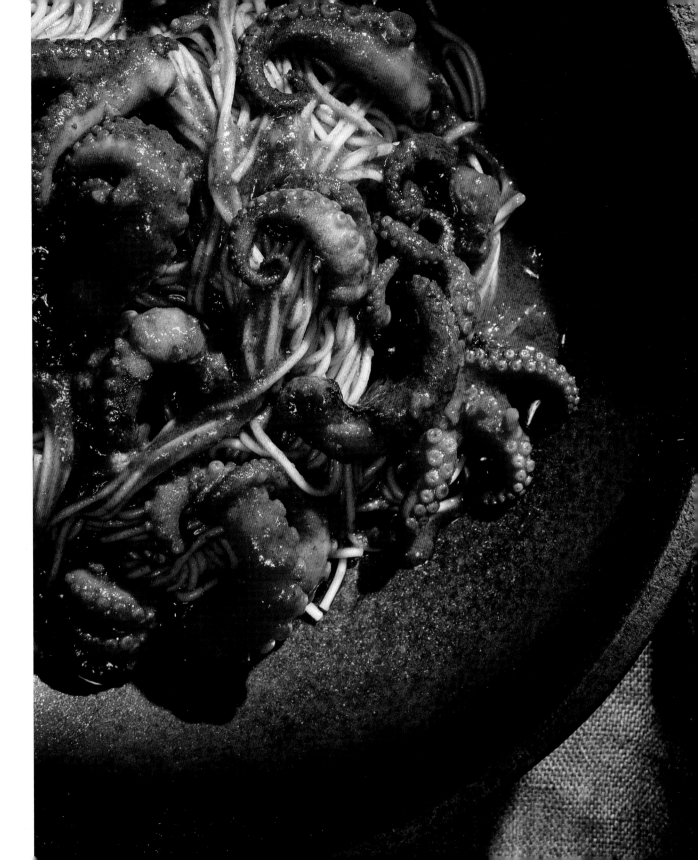

Leftover Salmon Surprise

SERVES 1
PREP TIME: 5 MINUTES
COOK TIME: 15 TO 20 MINUTES

2 cups (272 g) leftover cooked salmon or 1 can (14-ounce/397 g) salmon, drained

1 cup (170 g) leftover cooked rice

1 package (3 ounces/85 g) instant ramen noodles (any flavor)

1 Soft-Boiled Egg (page 29), peeled and halved

This recipe was a regular one way before it blew up on TikTok. The TikTok version uses rice and salmon, but here I added ramen! Ramen over rice is amazing, and even better with the addition of the fish. Perfect!

1. In a medium microwave-safe bowl, break up the salmon with a fork and mix it into the rice.

2. Cover the bowl with a wet napkin and microwave for 5 minutes on high.

3. Cook the ramen noodles according to the package directions and mix in the seasoning packet.

4. Let the ramen sit for 1 to 2 minutes, then drain all but 2 to 3 tablespoons of water.

5. Add the salmon mixture and mix until combined.

6. Top the salmon dish with the egg and dig in!

Ramen Crab Legs

1 tablespoon (6 g) Creole seasoning

1 ramen shrimp seasoning packet

3 crab legs (approximately 1 pound/455 g)

1 package (3 ounces/85 g) instant ramen, miso flavor, such as Maruchan Gold Spicy Miso

Growing up, my mom always told me crabs, lobsters, and shrimp were bugs, and I shouldn't eat bugs! Ha. Imagine my surprise when I finally tried crab and found out how good it tasted. I absolutely love crab legs; they are so good! You can save time buying cooked crab meat and just reheating it, but I personally enjoy the sound of cracking legs. Any kind of ramen works here, but I personally like spicy miso ramen.

1. Pour about 3 inches (7.5 cm) of water into a large shallow skillet and add the Creole seasoning and the shrimp seasoning packet. Bring to a simmer over medium-high heat.

2. Add the crab legs and simmer until cooked through, about 4 minutes, then remove the skillet from the heat and set it aside.

3. In a small saucepan, bring 2 cups (475 ml) of water to a boil over medium-high heat and add the ramen noodles.

4. After exactly 3 minutes, remove the saucepan from the heat and stir in the miso seasoning packet.

5. Pour the ramen into a serving bowl.

6. Remove the crab legs from the liquid, crack, remove the meat, and add it to the ramen.

Actually Good Shrimp Ramen

SERVES 1
PREP TIME: 15 MINUTES
COOK TIME: 10 MINUTES

1 (125 g) bundle sōmen noodles

2 teaspoons olive oil

16 shrimp, peeled and deveined

Sichuan chili sauce

2 scallions, green part only, chopped

1 Korean Marinated Egg (page 31), peeled and halved

1 teaspoon Zhong sauce

½ teaspoon Mala spice mix

Shrimp ramen has always been gross to me, mainly because the seasonings don't taste like shrimp. It just tastes like a bunch of salt. So I figured I could make a good shrimp ramen! In this delicious recipe, I use good sauces from Fly by Jing, but any kind of Szechuan chili sauce or chili oil would work.

1. Cook the sōmen noodles according to the package directions and set them aside.

2. Heat the oil in a medium skillet over medium heat and add the shrimp. Sauté until they are pink and cooked through, about 6 minutes.

3. Add the Sichuan sauce and stir to coat the shrimp. Remove the skillet from the heat and add the noodles, tossing to combine.

4. Transfer the mixture to a serving bowl and top with the scallions.

5. Arrange the egg on the side of the bowl and top each half with ½ teaspoon Zhong sauce.

6. Sprinkle with the mala spice mixture and serve.

VEGETARIAN

CHAPTER 5

Mac and Cheese Ramen

4 packages (3 ounces/85 g each) ramen noodles (any flavor will do!)

FOR THE CHEESE SAUCE

2 tablespoons (15 g) all-purpose flour

½ teaspoon sea salt

¼ teaspoon seasoning salt, such as Lawry's (optional)

2 tablespoons (28 g) butter

1 cup (235 ml) whole milk

2 cups (225 g) shredded cheddar cheese

This recipe is the first ramen dish I made on TV. *Access Daily* invited me to whip up something tasty, and they ended up amazed at how simple and easy the recipe was to make. Mac and cheese is always a favorite for Thanksgiving, so I ramen-ified our family recipe!

1. Remove the noodles from the packaging and place them in a 9-inch (23 cm) square baking dish. Save the seasoning packets for another recipe.

2. Pour hot water over the ramen noodles, covering them halfway, and let them sit for 3 minutes to soften.

3. Strain out the water and set the noodles aside.

4. Preheat the oven to 350°F (180°C).

5. In a small bowl, mix the flour, sea salt, and seasoning salt (if using) and set it aside.

6. Place a medium saucepan over medium heat and melt the butter.

7. Whisk in the flour mixture until well combined. Continue cooking until the mixture is slightly browned, about 3 to 5 minutes.

8. Add the milk and whisk until the sauce is smooth.

9. Add the cheese and whisk until the sauce thickens, about 3 to 5 minutes. Don't let it boil!

10. Pour the sauce over the noodles, stirring to combine.

11. Top with the shredded cheese and bake for 25 minutes or until golden brown.

12. Remove the baking dish from the oven, let it sit for 10 minutes or until cool, and enjoy!

Ramen Grilled Cheese and Tomato Soup

TOMATO SOUP

1 teaspoon olive oil

½ small sweet onion, diced

2 celery stalks, chopped

1 teaspoon minced garlic

2 cups (475 ml) vegetable broth

1 can (28-ounce/794 g) diced tomatoes

1 can (6-ounce/170 g) tomato paste

1 tablespoon (2 g) Italian seasoning

Salt

Freshly ground black pepper

RAMEN GRILLED CHEESE

1 package (3 ounces/85 g) instant ramen
noodles (any flavor)

¼ cup (55 g) butter

2 American cheese slices

Who doesn't love grilled cheese? This creation was a college fave! My roommates ate this meal a lot when my turn for cooking rolled around.

To Make the Tomato Soup

1. Heat the oil in a medium saucepan over medium-high heat. Sauté the onion, celery, and garlic for 3 minutes. Add the broth, tomatoes (including the juice), tomato paste, and Italian seasoning and bring to a boil. Reduce the heat to low and simmer the soup for 15 minutes.

2. Remove the soup from the heat and purée in a blender until smooth, adding more broth if the soup is too thick.

3. Season with salt and pepper.

To Make the Ramen Grilled Cheese

1. Remove the noodles from the packaging and separate the block into two pieces of "bread." Place them on a deep plate big enough to hold both. Save the seasoning packets for another recipe.

2. Pour enough hot water onto the plate to cover the ramen halfway. Don't use too much; some noodles should still be hard enough to hold things together! Let sit for 5 minutes.

3. Melt the butter in a large skillet over low to medium heat.

4. Place one block of ramen in the skillet, soft side down, and top with the cheese slices. Cook until partly melted, about 2 minutes.

5. Top the cheese with the other ramen piece, soft side up, and flip the sandwich. Cook uncovered until browned, about 2 to 3 minutes.

6. Remove the sandwich from the skillet and serve with a bowl of tomato soup. Dip and enjoy!

Your Very Basic Cheesy Ramen (Manga-Inspired Ramen)

SERVES 1
PREP TIME: 5 MINUTES
COOK TIME: 15 TO 20 MINUTES

1½ cups (355 ml) water

1 package (3 ounces/85 g) instant ramen noodles (any flavor)

1 large egg

2 American cheese slices

This is by far my favorite easy cheesy ramen to date! The dish was made popular by a manga, and it blew up on TikTok. I added my own flair to it, and boom! Love it.

1. In a medium skillet, bring the water to a gentle boil over medium-high heat.

2. Break the ramen noodle block into two halves and place them into the water.

3. Add the dried veggies and half the seasoning packet to the skillet (save the rest for later).

4. Let the ramen cook until you can break the noodles apart with a fork or chopsticks—about 2 to 3 minutes, but use your best judgment.

5. Create a well in the center of the noodles and carefully crack in the egg.

6. Cover, reduce the heat to low, and cook for 1 to 2 minutes, until the egg white is opaque.

7. Add the cheese slices and let the dish cool before eating it right out of the skillet.

NOTE:
I like to eat this with kimchi and scallions for a little extra flavor! You can also sprinkle on the rest of the seasoning, depending on your preference.

Ramen Lasagna

2 packages (3 ounces/85 g each) instant ramen noodles (any flavor)

1 jar (650 ml) of pasta sauce (your choice)

2 cups (300 g) shredded mozzarella cheese

This is the recipe that completely changed my life. I was going through a tough time with my relationship coming to an end, and a comment popped up about making a ramen lasagna. So I did. My video got 20 million views within a week or two! I was asked on TV, and magazine articles were written about me. I've been interviewed multiple times because of this one delicious recipe! It will forever be my favorite. What does it taste like? Try it and find out!

1. Preheat the oven to 350°F (180°C).

2. Separate the ramen blocks in half, creating four thinner squares, and place two of them in an 8-inch (20-cm) square baking dish.

3. Top with one-third of the tomato sauce and ½ cup (60 g) of cheese, then repeat with two more ramen halves, sauce, and cheese.

4. Crumble any remaining ramen over the lasagna and sprinkle with the last 1 cup (120 g) of cheese.

5. Bake the lasagna for 45 minutes until bubbly.

TIP:
Feel free to add vegetables, cottage cheese, or any other type of ingredient you like—there's no right or wrong way to do it.

SERVES 1
PREP TIME: 10 MINUTES
COOK TIME: 10 TO 15 MINUTES

Gluten-Free Ramen

1 (2.8-ounce/80 g) package red miso rice ramen noodles

1 package (16-ounce/475 ml) mushroom chicken bone broth

1 large baby bok choy, base cut off and roughly chopped

8 shiitake mushrooms, chopped

1 Soft-Boiled Egg (page 29), peeled and halved

I have a lot of friends who are gluten-free, so I had to include a couple recipes that they could eat. The noodles are a different texture than wheat-based noodles, but they are just as good if you make them correctly! If you don't you stir them constantly, they can stick together and become a gooey mess, but adding a little extra water can help avoid this problem.

1. In a small saucepan, bring 3 cups (711 ml) of water to a boil over medium-high heat and add the ramen noodles. After exactly 3 minutes, remove the saucepan from the heat, drain, and arrange the cooked noodles in a serving bowl.

2. In a medium skillet over medium heat, add the broth, bok choy, mushrooms, and seasoning packet. Bring the mixture to a simmer and cook 2 to 3 minutes or until the veggies are tender.

3. Using a ladle, top the ramen with the veggies. Ladle some of the broth around and top with the egg.

Watermelon Steak Ramen

1 (1-inch/2.5-cm) thick seedless watermelon slice, rind removed

½ teaspoon soy sauce

¼ teaspoon liquid smoke

¼ teaspoon minced garlic

¼ teaspoon lemon-garlic seasoning

⅛ teaspoon salt

⅛ teaspoon chili powder

1 teaspoon olive oil

1 package (3 ounces/85 g) instant ramen noodles (any flavor)

1 yellow zucchini, thinly sliced into disks

Balsamic vinaigrette, for drizzling

I made this recipe because my friend is a vegan, so she didn't eat steak. I wanted to see whether I could make watermelon taste like a steak, and I was surprised to find out that you can! I mean, if you're a meat eater, you know it's not as good as a steak, but it's a good alternative. Definitely try this one.

1. Season the watermelon on both sides with the soy sauce, liquid smoke, garlic, lemon-garlic seasoning, salt, and chili powder. Let the watermelon marinate for 5 minutes.

2. Heat the oil in a small skillet over medium heat. Pan-sear the watermelon for 2 to 3 minutes total, turning once, until lightly browned. Slice into thin strips.

3. While the watermelon is searing, place the zucchini in a microwave steamer with a couple tablespoons of water and steam for 1 minute. Set it aside. Alternatively, you can add 2 to 3 tablespoons (30 to 45 ml) of water to a pan and bring to a simmer. Then add the zucchini to the water, cover, and simmer for 3 to 4 minutes.

4. Cook the ramen noodles according to the package directions. Pour the cooked ramen and liquid into a serving bowl and add the seasoning packet.

5. Top the ramen with the watermelon slices and steamed zucchini. Drizzle it with balsamic vinaigrette and serve.

Dragon Fruit Ramen

4 red dragon fruit

1 package (3 ounces/85 g) instant ramen noodles, chicken flavor

¼ teaspoon powdered sriracha spice

½ teaspoon coconut oil

4 ounces (115 g) enoki mushrooms, ends cut off and discarded

2 teaspoons soy sauce

I'm constantly asked what dragon fruit tastes like, but it really doesn't have much of a taste. There are three different kinds: white dragon fruit which has no taste whatsoever in my opinion; red dragon fruit, which is a little tart, kind of sweet, and looks really cool; and yellow dragon fruit, which is the sweetest of the three!

1. Halve 3 of the dragon fruit, scoop the flesh into a plastic bag, and crush it until the fruit is a liquid-like pulp. Reserve one of the empty rinds and discard the rest. Slice the remaining dragon fruit thinly.

2. Pour the pulp into a medium skillet and heat over medium heat until bubbling.

3. Add the ramen noodles and cook until softened, about 3 minutes.

4. Remove the skillet from the heat, stir in the seasoning packet and sriracha spice, and set aside.

5. Melt the coconut oil in a small skillet over medium heat. Add the mushrooms, seasoning, and soy sauce, and sauté until tender, about 2 minutes.

6. Place the reserved dragon fruit rind in a serving bowl and scoop some of the noodles into the rind. Arrange the remaining noodles around the rind with spoonfuls of the broth.

7. Arrange dragon fruit slices for garnish on the side of the bowl. Top the ramen with the mushrooms and serve.

Pumpkin Ramen

1 small pie pumpkin

1 ramen seasoning packet (your choice)

Hot sauce

2 cups (475 ml) chicken broth

1 tablespoon (8 g) cornstarch

1 Soft-Boiled Egg (page 29), peeled and halved

This is a recipe requested by Tabasco. They wanted me to create a video using their sauces around Thanksgiving, so I took on the challenge and had a lot of fun. Feel free to substitute butternut squash or acorn squash for the pumpkin. You can save leftover toasted pumpkin seeds to top yogurts or chia seed puddings, or as a tasty snack.

1. Stem and halve the pumpkin. Scoop out the seeds, rinse, and pick through them to remove bits of pumpkin flesh.

2. Use a paper towel to pat dry the seeds, then place them into a bowl with the ramen seasoning packet and a generous splash of hot sauce. Stir to combine.

3. Transfer the seeds to an air fryer basket and air fry or place on a baking sheet in the oven for 25 to 30 minutes at 350°F (180°C). Remove the seeds and let them cool. Store any unused seeds in a sealed container at room temperature for up to 1 week.

4. Remove the pumpkin skin, cut one-half the pumpkin into wedges, and spiralize it. Place the "noodles" in a serving bowl.

5. Cut the remaining pumpkin half into two quarters. Thinly slice one quarter lengthwise and set aside. The remaining quarter can be used in another recipe.

6. In a medium saucepan, bring the chicken broth to a boil over medium heat.

7. Remove ½ cup (120 ml) of hot broth to a small bowl and whisk in the cornstarch.

8. Add the mixture back to the saucepan, whisking to thicken, about 2 minutes. Add a splash of hot sauce.

9. Pour the hot broth over the pumpkin noodles and set them aside to soften, about 5 minutes.

10. Garnish the dish with the pumpkin slices, the egg, the toasted pumpkin seeds, and a drizzle of hot sauce.

NOTE:
You're going to need a veggie spiralizer for this recipe.

Kiwi Ramen

5 kiwis, 4 halved, 1 thinly sliced

½ cup (120 ml) water

1 package (3 ounces/85 g) instant ramen noodles, chicken flavor

1 small pineapple, rind cut off and thinly sliced into rings

1 Soft-Boiled Egg (page 29), peeled and halved

Kiwi is delicious! I don't know why people freak out whenever I eat the skin, because it is completely edible. Plus, leaving the skin on makes much less of a mess. But I admit this broth is not the usual one for ramen, and it is a bit of an acquired taste. One of my followers suggested I try a kiwi-based dish, and I was up for the challenge. It's a meal to make when you're in the mood to play with your food—chunky broth and all—and quite tasty, in my opinion.

1. Place the halved kiwis and water in a blender and blend until smooth.

2. Pour the liquid into a small skillet and bring to a simmer over medium heat.

3. Add the ramen noodles and seasoning packet and cook until softened, about 3 minutes.

4. Pour the ramen into a serving bowl and arrange the pineapple and kiwi slices around the edges.

5. Top with the egg and serve.

Thai Chili
Rice Cake Surprise

1 package (3 ounces/85 g) instant ramen noodles, soy flavor

2 teaspoons (10 ml) olive oil

1 package (290 g) tteokbokki Korean rice cakes with sweet chili sauce

1 Soft-Boiled Egg (page 29), peeled and halved

2 scallions, white and green parts, chopped

Thai chili sriracha, for drizzling

I'd never used green sriracha before this recipe, and I wasn't sure I'd like it. Four in the morning seemed like a good time to experiment with leftover ingredients, and this tasty recipe was the result. The Thai chili sauce went perfectly with the spiciness of the rice cakes. If you don't have soy ramen noodles, a splash of soy sauce is perfectly fine to create the flavor.

1. Remove the noodles from the packaging and place them in a medium bowl.

2. Pour hot water over the noodles, covering them halfway, and let them sit for 3 minutes to soften.

3. While the noodles are softening, heat the oil in a medium skillet over medium-high heat and add the rice cakes and sauce. Stir for 2 to 4 minutes until heated through.

4. Add the ramen and liquid to a serving bowl and stir in the seasoning packet.

5. Arrange the rice cakes on one side and arrange the egg on the other.

6. Top with scallions and a drizzle of sriracha and serve.

Late-Night Ramen

1 package (120 g) spicy instant ramen, such as Shin spicy noodle soup

2 scallions, white and green parts, chopped

2 Soft-Boiled Eggs (page 29), peeled and halved

10 medium radishes, all colors, washed

Salt

Freshly ground black pepper

One day, I was watching a video on TikTok of a bunch of kids who were eating super spicy food and dipping radishes in the sauce. My mouth started watering immediately, and I had to get some of that crunch. The ramen I tried it with didn't have a thick sauce, but dipping those vegetables in the broth worked just fine. Somehow, the heat in the radishes smoothed out the spice of the other ingredients. Another successful experiment playing with food!

1. Bring 3½ cups (828 ml) of water to a simmer in a large saucepan over medium-high heat. Stir in the sauce packets and seasonings from the noodles, then add the noodles and cook according to the package instructions.

2. Pour the ramen in a medium serving bowl and add the eggs.

3. Garnish the ramen with the scallions and a drizzle of sriracha.

4. Place the whole radishes in a small serving bowl and season with salt and pepper.

5. Enjoy!

Kimchi Ramen

1 package (3 ounces/85 g) instant ramen noodles, kimchi flavor

1 package (180 g) kimchi dumplings

1 Soft-Boiled Egg (page 29), peeled and halved

Sriracha sauce, for drizzling

Somebody asked me to make kimchi ramen, and I took them up on the challenge. Walking around the store, I caught sight of kimchi dumplings and thought, *Ooh, that'll make it a little bit different*! Dumplings look so good when you pull them apart, and these complemented the ramen well. This recipe is amazing, and the soft-boiled egg just takes the flavor over the top. A scoop of jarred or homemade kimchi would be nice if you can't find the dumplings.

1. In a small saucepan, bring 2 cups (475 ml) of water to a boil over medium-high heat and add the ramen noodles. After 5 minutes, remove the saucepan from the heat and drain.

2. Transfer the ramen to a medium serving bowl and add sauce and seasoning packets and stir.

3. Prepare the dumplings following the package directions.

4. Arrange the dumplings on the ramen.

5. Top with the egg and a drizzle of sriracha.

Boba Ramen, Baby!

1 cup (152 g) tapioca pearls (I used WuFuYuan, Black Sugar flavor)

1 (125 g) bundle sōmen noodles

1 tablespoon (20 g) honey

2 chicken ramen seasoning packets

1 Soft-Boiled Egg (page 29), peeled and halved

Hot sauce, for drizzling

When I get boba tea, it's basically boba in a cup—barely any tea. While drinking (eating?) my beverage one day, I wondered whether boba pearls would absorb ramen broth and taste like ramen. So I tried it, and this recipe is delicious. I added honey to the boba to enhance their sweetness and cut the saltiness from the seasoning packet. Next time, I'm adding popping boba to the ingredient list!

1. Heat 2 cups (475 ml) of water in a medium saucepan over medium-high heat. Add the tapioca pearls and simmer for 5 minutes.

2. Strain the pearls and transfer them to an ice bath.

3. In another medium saucepan, heat 2 cups (475 ml) of water over medium-high heat. Add the sōmen noodles to the second saucepan and cook them according to the package directions.

4. Transfer the noodles and liquid to a medium serving bowl and stir in 1 seasoning packet.

5. Transfer the tapioca pearls to a small bowl and stir in the honey and the other seasoning packet.

6. Top the noodles with the tapioca pearls, the egg, and a drizzle of hot sauce.

Curry Ramen

1 package (3 ounces/85 g) instant ramen noodles, spicy curry flavor

1 package (180 g) broccoli dumplings

1 Soft-Boiled Egg (page 29), peeled and halved

Sriracha sauce, for drizzling

Curry ramen tastes amazing. I would have added extra curry powder or paste if I had any in my cupboards. This recipe is vegetarian, topped with broccoli dumplings, but any other ones would be great. If you do boost the flavor with more hot curry, skip the sriracha or you might need a gallon of water to cool down.

1. In a small saucepan, bring 2 cups (475 ml) of water to a boil over medium-high heat and add the ramen noodles. After 5 minutes, remove the saucepan from the heat and stir in the sauce and seasoning packet.

2. Transfer the ramen to a serving bowl.

3. Microwave the dumplings following the package directions.

4. Arrange the dumplings on the ramen.

5. Top with the egg and a drizzle of sriracha.

Yuzu Ramen

7 ounces (201 g) enoki mushrooms, ends trimmed off, separated, and washed

1 (500 ml) bottle blk. water (optional)

2 tablespoons (28 ml) olive oil

1 package (6-ounce/170 g) instant ramen, yuzu flavor, such as Itsuki Yuzushio

2 scallions, white and green parts, chopped

1 Soft-Boiled Egg (page 29), peeled and halved

I love enoki mushrooms, but for some reason, when I go to the store, I often can't find them. So whenever I see these beauties, I grab a bunch and then need recipes to use them up, like this one. Try the cooking technique here for the mushrooms and enjoy them as a tasty snack. You won't be disappointed.

1. Place the mushrooms in a medium bowl and pour the water over them, or cover them with regular water. Let the mushrooms soak for a minimum of 30 minutes (until they soak up the color of the water, if using blk. water).

2. Heat the oil in a medium skillet over medium-high heat and add the mushrooms and soaking liquid. Sauté until tender and golden, about 5 minutes. Remove the skillet from the heat and set it aside.

3. Bring 2 cups (475 ml) of water to a simmer in a small skillet over medium-high heat. Add the ramen noodles and cook them according to the package directions.

4. Ladle about 1 cup (235 ml) of the ramen cooking liquid into a medium serving bowl and stir in the seasoning packet.

5. Pour in the cooked noodles and remaining liquid, stirring to combine.

6. Top with the scallions, cooked mushrooms, and egg.

SIDES & SNACKS
CHAPTER 6

Ramen Pizza

2 packages (3 ounces/85 g each) instant ramen noodles (any flavor)

2 large eggs

1 jar (13-ounce/370 g) pizza sauce

1 package (11.25-ounce/320 g) shredded mozzarella

1 package (4-ounce/115 g) sliced pepperoni

Pizza seasoning

People freaked out—in both good and bad ways—when I set out to make ramen pizza. It isn't real pizza, apparently, but since it tastes like it, who cares if the crust is made of ramen? It's the perfect choice if you don't have a premade crust or dough handy in your freezer. Obviously, any toppings work, so go crazy and play with your food!

1. Place the ramen noodles in microwave-safe bowls or rapid ramen cookers with ½ cup (120 ml) of water and microwave each for 3 minutes. Stir to break up the noodles and drain. Save the seasoning packets for another recipe.

2. Crack 1 egg into each bowl and stir to combine.

3. Spread a large piece of foil—larger than the pizza stone or baking tray you'll be using—on your work surface and pour both bowls of ramen noodles into the middle of it.

4. Using a wooden spoon, spread the noodles out into a circle the same size as your baking surface. Refrigerate for 30 minutes to firm it up.

5. Preheat the oven to 350°F (180°C).

6. Transfer the ramen crust to a pizza stone or baking tray and spread the pizza sauce all over it, right to the edges. Top with shredded cheese, covering the entire surface. Arrange the pepperoni on the pizza and sprinkle with the pizza seasoning.

7. Bake the pizza for 25 to 30 minutes, until the cheese is bubbly and the ramen crust is crunchy.

Ramen Poutine

½ package (650 g) frozen french fries, extra-crispy crinkle variety

1 package (3 ounces/85 g) instant ramen noodles, chicken flavor

1 container (12-ounce/355 ml) beef gravy

½ cup (115 g) bacon, chopped

1 cup (225 g) fresh cheese curds or 1 container (16-ounce/475 ml) cheese dip, such as Gordo's, heated

I got yelled at for making this one, too. I didn't add cheese curds—mainly because I couldn't find them in the store—so I used cheese dip instead. If cheese curds are available where you live, make sure you add them, 1,000 percent! But feel free to have fun with his recipe; there's no right or wrong way to cook anything, it's all about making it the way you enjoy it. If you want to add ground beef on top, add ground beef; If you want chicken, add chicken! Have fun!

1. Spread the fries over three-quarters of a large air fryer basket and cook until crispy at 350°F (180°C) for 25 minutes, or bake on a baking sheet in the oven at the same temperature for 30 minutes.

2. While the fries are cooking, put the ramen noodles in a medium bowl and cover them with hot water. Let the noodles sit for 3 minutes to soften, then strain out the water. Save the seasoning packets for another recipe.

3. Heat the gravy in a small skillet over medium heat until bubbling, then reduce the heat to low and keep the gravy warm until the fries are done.

4. Place the fries in a serving bowl and sprinkle with the bacon. Top the fries with the drained ramen and hot gravy.

5. Heat the cheese dip according to the container directions and drizzle it over the fries, or top with cheese curds, if using.

TIP:
The toppings for this recipe are all about personal preference. Add as much bacon and cheese curds as you like!

Ramen Burrito

1 bag (9.9-ounce/280 g) spicy tortilla chips, such as Takis Fuego

1 package (3 ounces/85 g) instant ramen noodles (any flavor)

1 jar (16-ounce/475 ml) pizza sauce

1 can (4½-ounce/125 g) smoked sardines in olive oil

1 bag (11¼-ounce/320 g) shredded mozzarella cheese

½ cup (120 ml) water

2 tablespoons (28 g) mayonnaise

2 tablespoons (28 ml) sriracha sauce

1 Soft-Boiled Egg (page 29), peeled and chopped

This recipe is adapted from that prison cookbook (see page 34). It is as basic as it gets—just choose your ingredients and throw them in the bag. You can do it with a bunch of people, everyone choosing whatever they want. Every time I do one of these, people go crazy. The trick to getting the right texture is eyeballing the amount of water. Start with the amount in the recipe, and after scrunching it around in the bag, add more if the mixture is too dry. You want it to feel like thick cooked oatmeal.

1. Crush the tortilla chips in the bag and open one end.

2. Crumble the ramen noodles into the bag

3. Pour in the pizza sauce, sardines with oil, mozzarella, and water.

4. Fold the top of the bag down and clip it shut to create a sealed package. Put it in the refrigerator for at least 30 minutes.

5. In a small bowl, mix the mayonnaise, sriracha, and the egg with a fork until well blended.

6. Open the packet and serve topped with the sauce.

MAKES 8
PREP TIME: 15 MINUTES, PLUS 3
MINUTES FIRMING UP TIME
COOK TIME: 30 MINUTES

Ramen Onion Rings

2 packages (3 ounces/85 g each) instant ramen noodles, beef flavor

2 large eggs

1 package (9-ounce/255 g) onion ring batter mix

Olive oil, for frying

Your choice of dipping sauces (I like Chick-fil-A sauce and sriracha)

This is a really fun recipe that my followers asked me to make. I really had no idea what to do, but when I found a mini silicone donut mold, I said, "Perfect!" You can use any kind of mold, like a muffin tin or a popsicle mold—just make sure whatever you use is oven-safe! I like WhistleStop onion ring batter, but any kind will work.

1. Crush the ramen noodles and place them in a medium bowl. Pour hot water over the ramen noodles, covering them halfway, and let them sit for 5 minutes to soften. Drain.

2. Add the eggs and seasoning packets to the softened noodles, stirring to combine.

3. Transfer the mixture to a mini donut mold. Let sit at room temperature until the rings are firm, about 3 minutes.

4. In a medium bowl, prepare the batter mix according to the package directions. The batter should be thick.

5. When the rings are firm, heat 2 to 3 inches (5 to 7.5 cm) of oil in a medium saucepan over medium heat until it is 350°F (180°C).

6. Working in batches, remove the ramen rings from the mold and dredge them in the batter. Fry the rings, turning once, until golden brown and crispy, about 4 minutes total.

7. Drain the rings on paper towels and repeat until all the rings are cooked. Enjoy with your favorite condiments!

Spicy Ramen Cheesy Ball

1 to 1½ cups (110 to 165 g) spicy tortilla chips

1 package (3 ounces/85 g) instant ramen noodles (any flavor)

1 large egg

1 package (8-ounce/227 g) fresh mozzarella (preferably one large ball)

Olive oil, for frying

Here's another recipe suggested by one of my followers! I was confident I could make this one easily. Any kind of mozzarella and tortilla chips will work—I just grabbed the first ones I found in the store, but feel free to use your favorites! Galbani mozzarella is good because it has a spectacular cheese pull!

1. Crush the tortilla chips in a blender and transfer to a small bowl.

2. Crush the ramen noodles in the blender and transfer to a second small bowl.

3. Crack the egg into a third small bowl and beat with a whisk or fork.

4. Dredge the cheese in the egg, then the tortilla chips, then the egg again, and finally in the ramen noodles until well coated.

5. Heat 2 to 3 inches (5 to 7.5 cm) of oil in a medium pot over medium heat until it is 350°F (180°C).

6. Fry the breaded ball, turning once, until golden and crispy, about 5 minutes total.

Ramen Corn Dog

1 cup (140 g) fine yellow cornmeal

¾ cup (90 g) flour

¼ cup (50 g) sugar

1 teaspoon baking powder

½ teaspoon salt

1 cup (235 ml) milk

1 large egg

1 package (3 ounces/85 g) instant ramen noodles, chicken flavor

Olive oil, for frying

1 large or 2 regular hot dogs (beef, turkey, chicken), cut into 4-inch (10 cm) pieces

Mustard

Chick-fil-A sauce

I had a lot of fun with this recipe. I love corn dogs, so I really wanted to make one with ramen. I tried it multiple times before I got the batter right—it was too thick, too thin, then it wouldn't stick to the hot dog! You don't have to use a particular type of hot dog; whatever works for you is fine. But remember to have fun playing with your food.

1. In a medium bowl, whisk together the cornmeal, flour, sugar, baking powder, and salt until well blended.

2. Add the milk and egg, whisking to make a thick, smooth batter.

3. Crush the ramen noodles in the bag and transfer them to a plate. Save the seasoning packet for another recipe.

4. Pour 2 to 3 inches (5 to 7.5 cm) of oil in a large saucepan and heat to 350°F (180°C) over medium heat.

5. Insert wooden skewers into the hot dog pieces lengthwise.

6. Pour the batter into a large drinking glass, about three-quarters full, and dip the hot dogs straight into batter, swirling to fully coat. Shake off the excess.

7. Roll the corn dogs in the crushed ramen until coated.

8. Fry until golden brown on all sides, turning, 3 to 5 minutes total. Serve with mustard and Chick-fil-A sauce.

Ramen Spring Rolls

1 package (3 ounces/85 g) instant ramen noodles, chicken flavor

Canola oil or other vegetable oil, for frying

8 spring roll wrappers

1 hot dog, cut in half and cut into 1½-inch (4 cm) sticks

1 mozzarella string cheese, cut into ¼-inch by 1½-inch (6 mm by 4 cm) sticks

Chick-fil-A sauce

Sriracha sauce

Let me be honest: this recipe was designed to catch my viewers' attention. I chose hotdogs and mozzarella cheese as a filling because I wanted to see how those ingredients worked. Your spring rolls could use chicken and veggies like shredded carrots, bean sprouts, or snow peas.

1. Put the ramen noodles and seasoning packet in a medium bowl and cover them with hot water. Let the noodles sit for 3 minutes to soften, then strain out the water.

2. Place a spring roll wrapper on your work surface and arrange 2 tablespoons of ramen noodles diagonally from corner to corner.

3. Add 2 hot dog pieces, 2 pieces of cheese, and a drizzle of sauce.

4. Fold one corner of the spring roll wrapper over the filling and then fold over the sides. Roll the remaining side to create a cylinder.

5. Brush the edge of the wrapper with water and seal.

6. Repeat with the remaining wrappers.

7. Pour 2 to 3 inches (5 to 7.5 cm) of oil into a large saucepan and heat to 350°F (180°C) over medium heat.

8. Working in batches, fry the spring rolls until golden brown on all sides, about 2 minutes.

9. Drain the spring rolls on paper towels and repeat until all the rolls are cooked. Serve with the sauces.

Ramen Deviled Eggs

2 packages (3 ounces/85 g) instant ramen noodles, chicken flavor

9 large eggs

¼ cup (60 g) mayonnaise

1 teaspoon salt, or to taste

1 teaspoon coarsely ground black pepper, or to taste

Paprika

I was in a grocery store around Easter, and I saw a silicone mold in the shape of an egg. Immediately, I thought, *Why not make a ramen deviled egg?* I figured it would look cool on camera, and I wasn't wrong. If you like deviled eggs and you like ramen, this is the recipe for you!

1. Preheat the oven to 350°F (180°C).

2. Crush the ramen noodles in both packages and place them in a bowl. Set the seasoning packets aside.

3. Add 1 cup (235 ml) of water to the noodles and let them soften for 3 minutes.

4. Add 2 eggs to the softened ramen and stir to combine.

5. Spoon the mixture into Easter egg molds, smoothing out the tops, and bake until golden, about 5 to 10 minutes. Set them aside until cool.

6. While the ramen eggs are baking, place the remaining 7 eggs in a medium saucepan and cover them with cold water by about ½ inch (1 cm). Bring to a boil over medium-high heat and let boil for 1 minute.

7. Remove the saucepan from the heat and drain. Cover the eggs with cold water.

8. When they're cool, peel the hard-boiled eggs and place them in a medium bowl. Smash them with a fork and stir in the mayonnaise, salt, and pepper.

9. Remove the baked ramen eggs from the molds and top them with a generous scoop of egg salad. Sprinkle the topped eggs with the reserved seasoning packets and paprika.

COOKING WITH FRIENDS RECIPES

CHAPTER 7

The Struggle Meal That Struggles!

SERVES 2
PREP TIME: 15 MINUTES
COOK TIME: 15 MINUTES

1 tablespoon (15 ml) olive oil

1 small sweet onion, halved and sliced

2 baby bok choy, ends cut off and greens chopped

2 packages (120 g) spicy instant ramen, such as Shin spicy noodle soup

½ package (500 g) gyoza (I used Trader Joe's pork variety)

3 scallions, white and green parts, chopped

2 Soft-Boiled Eggs (page 29), peeled and halved

Sriracha sauce, for drizzling

My cooking partner for this recipe is Sue Ellen, an artist living in Los Angeles. Like most people I've met in this city, we first crossed paths in a coffee shop. She's super funny and very talented. I asked Sue Ellen to be my first guest on my "Cooking with Friends" series, and lucky for us, she said yes!

1. Heat the oil in a medium skillet over medium-high heat and sauté the onions until softened, about 3 minutes.

2. Add the bok choy and sauté until it is wilted, about 2 minutes. Remove the skillet from the heat and set it aside.

3. Bring 3½ cups (828 ml) of water to a simmer in a large saucepan over medium-high heat. Stir in the sauce packets and seasonings for the ramen and then add the noodles. Let them simmer for about 2 minutes, until softened.

4. Add the dumplings and simmer until they are softened and heated through, about 3 to 4 minutes.

5. Add the cooked veggies to the noodle mixture and stir to combine.

6. Divide the mixture between two bowls and top with chopped scallions, an egg, and a drizzle of sriracha on each.

Trojan Meal

Oil spray

6 large eggs, beaten

3 tomatoes, cut into eighths and each wedge cut in half width-wise

Salt

1 package (8.8-ounce/250 g) prepared basmati rice, such as Uncle Ben's

Meet Zoe! She's a YouTube content creator who specializes in growth-related content like fashion and healing diaries. When shooting this episode, she was also a self-described tech girly, working with a company named Honey. Zoe warned me she hadn't made this recipe in a while, but I was super excited to try it. She named it the Trojan Meal because the color matched the USC Trojans.

1. Heat a large nonstick skillet over medium heat and spray it with oil.

2. Pour the eggs into the skillet and let them sit undisturbed until they start to set.

3. Using a rubber spatula, gently scrape the set eggs to the center of the skillet from the edges, creating fluffy curds and allowing the uncooked egg to flow underneath.

4. Repeat this process until all the eggs are fluffy, still-moist curds, about 3 minutes.

5. Transfer the eggs to a medium bowl and set them aside.

6. Add the tomatoes to the skillet, season lightly with salt, and sauté until they break up a little and purge liquid, about 4 minutes. Cover the skillet and continue to heat while you make the rice.

7. Prepare the rice according to the package directions. Divide the rice between two plates.

8. Add the eggs back to the skillet, stirring to combine, and then scoop the mixture onto the rice.

Watch the full video here

Alexi's Greek-Style Eggs with Greens

SERVES 1

PREP TIME: 20 MINUTES

COOK TIME: 10 MINUTES

3 tablespoons (45 ml) olive oil, divided

1 small sweet onion, halved and thinly sliced

1 clove garlic, chopped roughly

½ bunch swiss chard, de-ribbed and greens chopped

3 large eggs, beaten

Salt

¾ cup (90 g) shredded cheese (cheddar or mozzarella), divided

3 small carrots, washed and julienned

1 small tomato, cut into eighths

1 small cucumber, cut into sticks and halved lengthwise

1 medium radish, thinly sliced

1 small scallion, julienned lengthwise

5 or 6 pitted kalamata olives

1 small apple, seeded and cut into eighths

1 lemon

I met Alexi Stavrou at his coffee shop in Hollywood. "Hey how are ya? Get yourself a coffee, best coffee in town!" he bellowed out his shop. Strange, but I approached him anyway, and he was right—Alexi serves one of the best Greek-style coffees I've ever had. He's also an actor who's appeared on television and is a big celebrity back home. You can make this recipe with anything in your fridge, but Alexi's version is spectacular, so follow along!

1. Heat 2 tablespoons (30 ml) of the oil in a large skillet over medium heat. Add the onion and garlic and sauté until softened, about 4 minutes.

2. Add the swiss chard greens (use the stalks in another recipe) and sauté until wilted, about 4 minutes.

3. Add the eggs, stirring to combine, until the eggs are cooked through, about 2 minutes. Season with salt to taste.

4. Sprinkle in the cheese, stir to combine, and arrange the eggs and greens on half of a plate.

5. Arrange the carrots, tomato, cucumber, radish, and scallions on the other half of the plate and drizzle with the remaining 1 tablespoon (15 ml) of olive oil.

6. Season the salad with salt to taste and top with the olives.

7. Arrange the apple wedges beside the salad and squeeze fresh lemon juice all over everything!

Colombian Happy Place

SERVES 1
PREP TIME: 10 MINUTES
COOK TIME: 20 MINUTES

Olive oil, for frying

2 green plantains, peeled and sliced

¾ cup (100 g) queso fresco

Oil spray

2 large eggs

Allow me to introduce you to Maria Legarda, a content creator and actor who took over to my studio to make her struggle meal! This dish is one she eats frequently (and did even more while in college). When I tell you it's amazing, it is seriously *amazing*! Side note: she challenged me in an episode of *Budget Meals* . . . and whooped my butt!

1. Heat 2 to 3 inches (5 to 7.5 cm) of oil in a medium saucepan over medium heat until it is 350°F (180°C).

2. Fry the plantain slices in batches until they are golden, about 2 minutes. Transfer the slices with a slotted spoon to a plate lined with paper towels to drain.

3. Arrange the slices on a serving plate and crumble two-thirds of the cheese all over them. Set the plate aside.

4. Heat the oil in a small nonstick skillet over medium-high heat.

5. Carefully crack the eggs into the skillet, keeping the yolks intact. Fry the eggs undisturbed until the whites are almost set but there is still liquid around the yolk, about 2 minutes.

6. Flip the eggs over gently, still with the yolks intact. Let the eggs fry about 10 seconds, flip them over again, and slide them onto the cheesy plantains.

7. Top with the remaining cheese and serve!

On a Weekend

1 package (120 g) spicy instant ramen, such as Shin spicy noodle soup

1 large egg

1 teaspoon sesame oil

This recipe creator is Clement, a.k.a. the Ramen Guy. He's been making content since 2020, like most of us on the internet these days. He's based out of Canada and loves ramen as much as I do. Clement traveled all the way to LA to show me his struggle meal. It's a simple yet delicious journey to flavor-ville.

1. Heat 1 cup (235 ml) of water in a medium skillet over medium-high heat and bring to a simmer.

2. Stir in the sauce packet and seasoning from the noodles and then add the noodles. Let them simmer for about 2 minutes until softened.

3. Stir to disperse the noodles in the simmering broth.

4. Crack the egg into the skillet, turn off the heat, and stir until the egg is cooked, about 2 minutes.

5. Drizzle in the sesame oil and serve.

Dani 15

1 package (3 ounces/85 g) instant ramen noodles, chicken flavor

1 package (14-ounce/397 g) beef shaved steak

2 baby bella mushrooms, sliced

½ cup (60 g) shredded cheese (your preference)

3 scallions, white and green parts, chopped

Daniela Legarda is a content creator and actor who is doing big things in the social media space. She shared this struggle meal, and it's low-key a banger! You can substitute veggies or tofu in place of the meat if you want a meat-free option.

1. Heat 2 cups (475 ml) of water in a small saucepan over medium heat until simmering. Add the ramen noodles and simmer until softened, about 3 minutes.

2. Stir in the steak pieces and mushrooms and simmer until it they're cooked through, about 2 to 3 minutes.

3. Transfer the noodle mixture to a plate and sprinkle with the cheese, seasoning packet, and scallions.

Angry Struggle

2 packages (3 ounces/85 g) instant ramen noodles, chicken flavor

2 large eggs

1 teaspoon garlic powder

1 teaspoon Lawry's seasoning salt

Ritz crackers, for serving

Meet Oneya, a.k.a. Angry Reactions, which is misleading because he's known for uplifting videos and spreading some peace, love, and kindness on the internet. I remember watching his videos during 2020 and it's such a pleasure to meet the legend in person. Oneya's struggle meal is simple with a ton of flavor.

1. Heat 2 cups (475 ml) of water in a medium saucepan over medium-high heat until it is simmering.

2. Add the ramen noodles and simmer until softened, about 3 minutes. Transfer the noodles from the water to a medium bowl and set them aside.

3. Bring the water back to a boil and crack in the eggs. Poach the eggs until the whites are firm, about 3 minutes.

4. Add the seasoning packets, garlic powder, and seasoning salt to the noodles, stirring to combine.

5. Scoop the poached eggs out of the water with a slotted spoon and place them on top of the noodles. Pour the cooking water from the eggs over the noodles. Stir carefully so you don't break the eggs.

6. Serve with the Ritz crackers for dipping.

Acknowledgments

THANKS!

I want to thank each and every one of the RamFam for your continued support. I would not be where I am without you, and I'm honored to be a part of this community we created together.

I want to give a shout out to my mom for making me eat her style of ramen as a kid. Without this experience, I wouldn't have known I needed to perfect it and make it better. Ha ha! She is my biggest fan. Love you, Mom.

I also want to thank my dad for instilling in me how important it is to work hard at something you care about. I found it, Dad.

Of course, thanks to my siblings for growing up with me, always thinking I was weird, and knowing I would do something big.

Thank you so much, guys, and I hope you enjoy this cookbook.

About the Author

HEY!!! So my name is Ivan McCombs, but I'm better known as RamenKingIvan across the internet. I'm a regular guy who just loves playing with his food and it's brought me a support base of over 14 million followers! So crazy how life has changed for me and I owe it all to ramen and the interest of those who I call the RAMFAM. I am honored to present this book to you and I hope you get as much fun out of it as I had creating the recipes.

Index